Samurai Sales

Samurai Sales

The Modern Warrior's Guide to Selling

Jason Griffiths

iUniverse LLC
Bloomington

SAMURAI SALES
THE MODERN WARRIOR'S GUIDE TO SELLING

Copyright © 2014 Jason Griffiths.

All rights reserved. No part of this book may be used or reproduced by any means, graphic, electronic, or mechanical, including photocopying, recording, taping or by any information storage retrieval system without the written permission of the publisher except in the case of brief quotations embodied in critical articles and reviews.

iUniverse books may be ordered through booksellers or by contacting:

iUniverse
1663 Liberty Drive
Bloomington, IN 47403
www.iuniverse.com
1-800-Authors (1-800-288-4677)

Because of the dynamic nature of the Internet, any web addresses or links contained in this book may have changed since publication and may no longer be valid. The views expressed in this work are solely those of the author and do not necessarily reflect the views of the publisher, and the publisher hereby disclaims any responsibility for them.

Any people depicted in stock imagery provided by Thinkstock are models, and such images are being used for illustrative purposes only.

Certain stock imagery © Thinkstock.

ISBN: 978-1-4759-8348-7 (sc)
ISBN: 978-1-4759-8349-4 (hc)
ISBN: 978-1-4759-8350-0 (e)

Library of Congress Control Number: 2013905718

Printed in the United States of America.

iUniverse rev. date: 5/07/2014

For Pamela Dorr, whose continuation of the work of Samuel Mockbee and the HERO project inspires ripples around the world.

Inspiration that inadvertently caused me to get off my backside and write this book.

How's that for a ripple?

For me, writing is an outlet allowing me to write my opinions through the voices of others. Who would have imagined them correct?

Jason

Contents

Preface	ix
Prologue	xvii
Prospecting	1
Focus and Punctuality	8
Consistency and Effort	15
Goal Setting	21
First Impressions	31
Commitment	33
Courage and Self-Control	34
DISC	41
Working a Room	51
Qualification	63
Tour	71
Patience	75
Enthusiasm	79
Determination and Follow-Through	96
Handling Objections	99
Preclose	107
Balance and Flexibility	109
Price Presentation	123
Close	131
Referrals	143
Perseverance	170
Samurai Sales	177
The Creed	186
Appendix A	187
Appendix B	191
Appendix C	193
Appendix D	197

Preface

Why write?

I guess *Samurai Sales* began with a chance meeting with a gentleman from Osaka, Japan, named Shinji Aramaki. I met Shinji at an overly air-conditioned Vancouver airport. He and I shivered, waiting three hours for our respective flights, east and west. It could be that my brain cells were freezing in place, but I maintain that it was most likely this chance encounter during which the premise for writing this book was most probably laid.

It was the kind of encounter where rapport is assumed before having been established, the kind where you're well into a conversation for over half an hour before you even think of asking each other's names. Our discussion that overcast afternoon led us to the mutual conclusions that everybody sells something or another, ranging from concrete to abstract articles, including the self. People sell themselves to prospective employers during interviews that they are right for the job, the best candidate to earn the business money.

Shinji and I talked with each other as only salespeople could (for apparently, as my colleagues in marketing would have me believe, salespeople use a secret language or some such thing). It was only a matter of practicality that our jobs would one day be obsolete. Someday, someone was bound to write a practical book that everybody could understand, and every fly-by-night sales trainer, life coach, consultant, and sales manager would be put out of a job.

One day someone would write a book that would practically reduce the necessity for sales trainers. We were grateful that such a written work didn't exist yet, though one day we were sure one would be.

Shinji (a.k.a. Jin) and I concluded that although teaching sales techniques to people was a valuable service, it was one that could be done better, especially for those with a less passionate desire to learn how to sell. For a long time during my sales career, there seemed not to be anything inspiring on learning how to sell, or how to sell better. Sales-training books plodded along with the occasional new addendum, but they were for the most part a shopping list of techniques: step one, smile; step two, ask; step three, listen; step four, close. Though I found works such as the Chicken Soup series and *Simplify Your Life* valuable tools in their own right, they failed to inspire me to do the one thing that needed to be done almost as much as programs such as *Simpleology* failed to do. Where was the romance? Where was the hope? Where was the plausibility of learning?

Perhaps nothing too advantageous had been written for the fear of eventually eliminating employment, as Shinji and I had discussed.

I and most salespeople of my generation grew up learning techniques from the works of greats such as Kenneth Blanchard and Zig Ziglar, including reading classics such as the entire One Minute series and *Gung Ho!* and pawing over the entire FISH! philosophy, even paying homage to the world-famous Pike Place Fish Market at Pike Place Market in Seattle. I have looked to the words of gurus ranging from the caliber of Anthony Robbins to the less illustrious Lance Gregorchuk for guidance; sometimes they're good, and sometimes they're not as good. Every turn's a learning curve.

I am of the opinion that people are still people. There will always be a demand for a more personal, or "human," touch and therefore employment and perhaps ego for every sales trainer, life coach, consultant, and sales manager need not feel threatened. However, during those "boring book times," it remained very frustrating not having new emotionally rich materials upon which to draw.

There's an old saying that frustration is a sign you're about to have a breakthrough. Well, that breakthrough had been waiting in me for over ten years. With knowledge expanding as quickly as it did, it seemed so implausible and borderline unacceptable to me that such a work had not yet been written. It occurred to me that if no one else was to take on the challenge, perhaps it was my turn to step up and create something new.

After fourteen years of teaching hundreds of companies[1] how to sell more effectively, it occurred to me that history might be waiting for me to write such a work and reach out to tens of thousands more people (if not, hopefully, hundreds of thousands more) and share my experiences and knowledge. I wanted to reach out to and emotionally connect with as many people as possible, teaching life skills and selling techniques that will lead people ultimately to a better quality of life. I felt and still feel that it is a worthy contribution. This was the guiding principle that motivated me to write *Samurai Sales*. I find it cool to connect with people viscerally.

An emotional connection happens through stories. Rock climbing was never as popular as it was until after Sylvester Stallone starred in *Cliffhanger*. I'm not under any delusions that *Samurai Sales* is going to motivate as many people as Sly Stallone was able to, but who knows? What makes *Samurai Sales* unique is that it is based

---

1   It's 213 at the time of writing this book, to be exact. I have no idea exactly how many people are within that sphere of influence. It includes companies such as Belgacom Telecommunications, CARÉ Broadband (now Verizon), and all UK-based Holmes Place Health Clubs in Germany, Switzerland, France, and Austria. Fitness chains such as FYZIX, and major clubs such as NRG Healthcentre in Belgium, have tripled revenues with the influence of just one one-day seminar.

on real-life experiences, in most cases my own. Everyone is the sum of their choices, and therefore each person's set of experiences is unique. Each unique sum of experiences offers a fresh point of view that I've chosen to share herein. It is my hope that by sharing my experiences (sometimes quite descriptively), readers will be encouraged to change in ways that better either themselves or their environment, both intuitively and instinctively.

I use stories to involve the reader on a personal level. I've collected them over the years and continue to use them in reference during my seminars. As far as *Samurai Sales* was concerned, it seemed all I had to do was string the stories together, take a writing course, take a typing course, write the story, approach the publishing companies (which I would later drop), rewrite the story about five or six times, get it printed, market it to distributors, get it properly published, and get it distributed.

Phew!

Gosh, I thought, *if that is all there is to be done, what on earth am I waiting for?*

I leave you, the reader, to be the judge of how well it's been done.

I have had the good fortune to have met many of the sales gurus of my time. However, it was only as a "martial arts activist" that I became painfully aware that there existed in me a deeper importance in inspiring the aspiring generation of the twenty-first century to actually learn through sharing my limited knowledge, whether they were good or not-so-good experiences. Leading by cheerful example and teaching, sharing, and inspiring others affected me on a very personal level in rural Greensboro, Alabama, during a project for which I am ever grateful to have been a part of. In a way, I still am involved. The teachings of Samuel Mockbee were shown to me by Pamela Dorr and were connected through my Ultimate Black Belt Test coach and good friend, Tom Callos.

Without them, I may have never had the courage or the audacity to write this book.

I felt the works of others were repeating the same old, same old, and they weren't reaching out to people other than those actively interested in selling or becoming salespeople. Though many have tried, I had found neither lecture nor book creatively inspiring great, universally valuable sales techniques since the nineties, and I needn't have contacted Nostradamus to predict what I was to embark upon.

Though I wanted to read something that would inspire me and possibly enrich me as a human being, there was nothing. However, this attitude might have been complimentary to the popular movement of the times ... I'd like to coin a title for that popular movement: the anti-salesperson movement. As best I can tell, the anti-salesperson had "evolved" into being around 2002 in Europe. A great resistance to becoming a good salesperson was apparent. I should point out that the anti-sales movement could just as easily be coined the "anti-anything" movement, because a generation of youth were not bothered either to work or do just about anything constructive when the loopholes in the system were so lucrative. This is a good thing, because the future will also need numerous people for menial labor.

Still, the truth remained that nobody likes the stereotypical salesperson, and certainly nobody wants to become someone whom nobody likes. The irony here is that everybody is a salesperson to some degree; it's simply a matter of understanding what it is that we sell.

I remain passionate about sales and everything related to the sales process. The truth is not so apparent that we all sell something. No matter what we do, we sell—it's the nature of the world's commerce. Even volunteers are subject to the truth of consumerism. By learning how to sell effectively and efficiently, we can all lead more productive and successful lives.

The greatest challenges for me as director of the European Health and Sports Association were in teaching people how to sell without having to call for a sales meeting or a sales seminar that nobody would go to anyway. Quite fortunately, the seminars I delivered consistently brought success to my clients, but I was troubled as to why they did. What was it about my seminars that led the employees to a successful result?

As I discovered, the answers were quite literally in story. It was the stories I told that people listened to; after all, who doesn't enjoy a good story we will all adhere to, hold on to? Our oldest memories are replayed in our mind's eye as a story; all I needed to do was move my storytelling from good to great, and the results would reflect that.

I suppose that *Samurai Sales* is a work that's been in progress for just over five years, after the aforementioned meeting in a Vancouver airport brought me to the conclusion that people generally learn best when taught in story form. Any child knows this to be true. What is surprising is that this form of instructional storytelling[2]

---

[2] Instructional storytelling is a phrase I've started using to describe a certain learning phenomenon. I'm confident the phrase isn't mine, but I haven't been able to find out to whom it belongs. We all listen best when we hear a good story. We all heed best when we are listening well enough. ... It stands to reason, then, that if I tell the most interesting story, then I can teach without ever giving that feeling of having sat in a classroom environment for hours. It was always the little jokes (some good, some not so good) that my senior physics and biology teacher, Geoff Campbell, told that kept the class listening—even if only to roll our eyes later at how poor the jokes were. The point is that we all attended class regularly, and I understand his classes' grade averages were significantly above the norm. I easily remember him sharing some of his of his methodology on becoming a better teacher, and I consider him one of my personal heroes for doing it. He constantly strives to become a better educator no matter how good he already is, and those values were installed in me in my mid-teens.

exists so rarely directly in my North American Caucasian culture as an adult. Yet we all remember the stories we like.

I tell Jin's tale in a story format so that the reader can empathize with the main character, if not relate to him. *Samurai Sales* is told in a format that will hopefully teach the lessons. The depth of my characters and tales themselves are reached based on my life's experiences relating to people I have known in both sales and management—though I'll never tell who's who in the story. If any of them are reading this book, I thank you for the experiences we've shared; you have enriched me as a person in some way and have allowed me to grow in directions I might not have otherwise been able to go.

Special notes of thanks go out to my family for trusting in me when no others would. Thank you, Dad, for teaching me I could do anything I wanted to do. Thanks, Mom, for even admiring my "gypsy heart" and my ability to pick up and go at the drop of a hat; thank you for bearing me and giving me the chance to breathe. Thank you, parents, for raising me with the virtues you have shown me through your example.

A hearty portion of thanks go out to my high school friends, Mark, Shad, Richard, and Glenn, for being so brutally honest with me and still accepting me for all my faults. Thanks to all my friends for buying my book; I think you were among the first thousand sold—either that, or my mom bought a lot more copies than she needed. A load of thanks go out to my good friends, and I am pleased to count among them Tom Callos and Uri Geller, without whom the writing of this book would never have been possible. All of you, and the special woman in my life, have inspired me to believe in myself to new heights, enabling me to take on the seemingly impossible. Thank you.

Samurai Sales may be used as a teaching tool in other businesses to inspire employees in the form of lectures (of which I have an e-format lecture, which I will gladly share for free to anyone who e-mails me), although I feel it is most effective when employees simply read Jin's story for themselves.

This work is meant to be the modern warrior's guide to sales. Jin's story is meant to be enjoyed for what it is, and to teach subconsciously the techniques necessary to become a great salesperson, whether it be to sell ourselves at our next job interview or to sell why we should get a better price on the next thing we purchase. Ultimately, it is my hope that through reading this book, readers will in some way utilize that "little difference" from the knowledge gained by reading this tale to enrich their lives. I sincerely hope it brings a smile or three across their face as they learn what Jin did.

What did Jin do? Well, read on and enjoy.

Prologue

Arrival

The Boeing's right wheel grabbed the blacktop first, clunking the 767 askew from the desired direction ever so slightly. An eerie silence went through the cabin.

Gravity released as the aircraft's industrial-strength shocks tested their limits. Stomachs clenched against the feeling normally expected at the top of amusement park rides; this time the experience was far from uplifting. Time seemed to slow down just enough to allow passengers to question whether or not the shocks would hold such an impact, and whether they were going to live through this. Eleven tons of jumbo jet began to slide before any passenger had time to draw his or her next breath.

So why was the passenger seated on the inside aisle of row 36 smiling as the heavyweight continued its three-wheel drift toward the Seattle airport? It had been a rocky flight from the get-go, Jin recalled. The copilot's stomping of the pedals left and right to adjust for the discovered turbulence had not been successful the first thirty minutes of flight, and it had not done much for the nerves of the passengers during the last half an hour. To his knowledge, the stomping techniques had been amended since a crash over New York a couple of years before, which caused a tail fin of a plane to shear off, making it impossible to recover. All passengers had perished.

The fingernails of Jin's neighboring passenger began to dig into his hands, and loose articles seemed to move as if in slow motion, or somewhere in orbit inside the cabin. The initial manicured pains subsided as Jin gave in to the moment's irrelevance, and he smiled to recapture a moment just a few days before: "I'm going tornado surfing!" The memory of that conversation completed Jin's smile well up into his cheekbones.

He was arriving in style! All three pieces of landing gear gleefully squealed like an uncontrollable toddler to announce his arrival! He could have laughed out but for the reminder of what he was leaving behind.

What was left behind included Jin's grandmother. Gran was known in the community as an exceptionally polite woman, always smiling, with her winter hair kept neatly to the back of her neck. Though frail in stature, Gran had a strength of character that made everything she did a little better than one would expect. Each time Jin got ready to greet the day, Gran would share this wisdom with him as a gentle reminder: "You're not fully dressed until you put your smile on." Even that day, his most woeful day, it would be necessary to do so, though his heart wasn't at all in it. He'd have to fake it until he made it. Habits were difficult to break, whether they were good habits or bad ones.

Jin's ritual began each day began with a regime of calisthenics, including one hundred crunches, one hundred press-ups, and a run-through of his martial arts forms, which got the blood flowing sharply and his attention span focused on what there was to do that day.

Today he'd be visiting family for the wake of his mother. It used to be he wasn't permitted breakfast until these rituals were completed, as well as teeth being brushed, his face being washed and clean shaven (a relatively new additional rite of passage), and his hair made presentable. It still eluded him how Gran always knew when he skipped on one or the other.

A lovely lady, Gran was brought up when the highest of standards of morality were enforced. A fallout in the village meant one's family might go hungry in the winter time. She lived by the standards of being honest through and through. The solemn peace created from living this way allowed Gran to perform her yoga at a level to which young Jin could aspire.

"You're just not fresh if you forgo any of your rituals," she'd say. "It may not always be possible to have fun all the time, but by choosing your attitude, you open yourself up to the possibility of humor discovering you. Be open for it and watch it come to you; you'll see."

The day seemed the longest of his life. It dragged on and on as he missed his mother more and more. Even later in the day, as friends of his mother arrived to pay their respects, their warmth felt misplaced though well intended.

Jin's cousin, Art, and he had grown up together. They'd been more brothers than cousins. After Jin's father left when Jin was still a baby, his uncle took Gran, mom, and Jin into his home while still in Japan. Uncle D's advertising business was very successful and had grown enough that he'd moved to the Americas four years ago. The transition was made easier by the fact that Uncle D had an American wife he'd met while she was on vacation visiting her homeland; they fell in love in a café they frequented at the base of Mount Fuji. Uncle D had to travel an hour each way to see her and came home smiling each day he saw "his little missus," claiming she'd one day be his Missus Kisses. They moved to Washington shortly after getting married, and it was a happy time for all. Gran took it on as her responsibility that everything went smoothly. She made sure all the families involved like each other. She seemed to have the knack to guide people in conversations, and she listened with such enthusiasm that it was impossible not to like her.

Art wasn't always taller than Jin. Art wore soft-spoken clothing even as a kid and didn't think much of brand-named clothing. He had the kind of hair cut that that made a person look like he was not at ease, and yet a person simply liked him the moment he was around. Less physically and more mechanically inclined, Art was by no means out of shape.

Like all good brothers, Art and Jin had fought. They were a year and a half apart in age, with Art being the senior sibling. The fact was, Art gave Jin his first broken nose after Jin chased him screaming bloody murder for something he could no longer remember; Art spun round with a closed fist and squarely connected, knocking Jin out cold. Art ran home to Jin's mom, crying all the way and thinking he'd killed him. He was too upset to say where Jin lay, and the entire family had to wait until Jin regained consciousness and walked in, still damp and cold from lying in the field where they'd been playing. Art was so happy to see him again that he threw his arms around him and professed how sorry he truly was; how much he loved him, his only brother; and how silly a thing it was to do. Then, upon realizing he was hugging the person he thought he'd killed just moments ago, Art fainted.

Today was just that day where Jin wanted to fall into mourning. Was he being disrespectful for not showing his compassion? Old wounds seemed to resurface in his memory, and everything about his mother seemed so perfect. Jin remembered the sternness in his mother's voice whenever discipline was required, the understanding and forgiveness when he disappointed her, and the caring and simplicity of her smile that seemed to come from somewhere else.

Jin's mother was always presentable, immaculately groomed. Being a single mom, she had kept her hair relatively short throughout Jin's childhood; apparently as a baby, Jin had a grip that he could hang from for nearly an hour, and he would do so as often as possible. She'd grown her hair out for many years as a statement of her son's coming of age.

Jin was at school when he heard of his mother slipping while carrying some groceries. Doctors explained to him that a broken milk bottle might cost his mother her arm. Panic set in immediately as Jin rushed to her, to see whether she was going to be all right. It seemed Jin held his breath for the next two days as the wound was examined, the glass was removed, the nerves were repaired, and the okay was given that the arm would regain mobility after some physiotherapy. Tears of relief flowed uncontrollably from Jin when his mother explained she was going to have to cut short her silver hair, because she wouldn't be able to raise her arm to wash and brush it.

At the wake, Jin just couldn't manage bringing himself to care what happened to him. Live or die—it all seemed so immaterial. He didn't care what happened to himself and felt he'd hit rock bottom. The forced courteousness and smiling weighed heavily.

The memory of his mother's having to cut off her long locks of silver was at the forefront of his mind, and at that moment Jin was able to express words from the deepest regions of his soul. "I cannot control my eyes, for they miss this loving person so very much." The welled tears released, and Jin's healing could begin.

Jin's move to America was a family decision made after the passing of his mother. Everyone involved felt it best that he get away from it all, at least for a while. As it was a bit of a snap decision, return flights for Uncle D and his family could not be scheduled together for Jin. Jin's cousin, Art, warned there'd been storm warnings. Still, Art promised, "I'll pick you up at the airport when you get in."

"Great," he said under his breath, "I'm going tornado surfing."

"Well, that at least sounds like fun," Art hesitantly offered and for the first time that day, humor found its way to Jin. He could both smile and weep wholeheartedly for all who had lost someone that day.

"When the worst is before you, and there's nothing else to do about it, smile the best you can and ride it out. It'll pass. One way or another; it will pass." Uncle D seemed to have carried on Gran's pool of wisdom for every occasion, even for occasions involving imminent disaster.

The funny thing about disaster situations was how well one's senses become heightened. Every moment seems so much more in focus. The mind records everything with a clarity and depth that would baffle Blu-Ray technology. The body becomes so finely tuned to its own functions that an outward sigh from the nostrils drowns out all else as it tickles over the top lip. The mind seems to have all the time in the world to make up random thoughts of comfort—not the least of which was where Jin's thoughtful trail blazed to acknowledge where he was.

The land of opportunity.

Well, this was most certainly the landing of opportunity! *Just ride it out. No matter how bad the situation is that you find yourself in, ride it out and get through it. Nothing stays bad forever.*

The lurch of the plane brought the passengers well back into their seats. It assured them the ride was over and they were okay, and Jin's senses returned to normal.

The plane pulled solemnly up to gate nineteen. After a small delay, the "Fasten safety belt" sign was switched off, and the pilot was understandably too shaken and not well enough to greet the passengers as they disembarked the plane. Passengers overheard the apparent need of some cleaners to be sent to the cockpit.

The airfield was heavily overcast, but no rain fell. It was the kind of day that could dampen the impact of the greatest of events, but not the least one's resolve to get on with it.

Jin would never mention the Richter-scaled landing to either his uncle or his cousin, because he could already imagine his uncle saying, "That which doesn't kill you can only make you stronger." It was enough for Jin to wonder how much stronger he would be made after his jumbo experience. *Strong enough to take on whatever life throws my way,* he reckoned. Perhaps Jin was even strong enough to land his own opportunities. That would be something!

It was time to go and meet with his relatives. Jin was grateful simply to be, and the Seattle airfield was as great place as any to start.

Prospecting

Both Near and Far

It was a long flight, and Jin was eager to get settled in as soon as possible. Respectful greetings were exchanged along with gifts wrapped in pink paper, traditionally symbolic of genuinely liking someone and wishing one well. The embraces seemed askew from character but were by no means unwelcome.

Although Jin was certain both his uncle and cousin were sincerely explaining to him the cultural differences he would now be facing, he had to admit to himself that he wasn't very receptive to their input. Grateful? Yes. Courteous? Yes. But receptive? No. He meant not the least disrespect to either of them, but he was struggling with both the jet lag and the adrenaline hangover from the flight. He needed to get into bed and sleep for a while—perhaps a week.

Uncle D was a man of stature but was not particularly tall; he was of average build and average means. His deep voice and honesty gave him a respectable agreeability, not unlike that of a Welshman. Uncle D never needed to raise his voice to let a person know he meant what he was saying, which was no doubt one of the reasons he had been quite successful in business.

Uncle D's advertising business was doing quite well, and as best Jin could make out from under his heavy eyelids, it was due to the extra levels of service that Uncle D's business provided. "It's not just what services you're offering, Jin," his uncle was saying. "It's the *attitude* behind those services. I entered the advertising market at a time when it seemed to most of my company's prospective customers that we were all essentially providing the exact same packages for about the same amount of money. No one was particularly interested, you see. Jin, do try to stay awake, son ... No one was interested because marketing had become increasingly more expensive with increasingly less yield.

"I was asked by one particular manager, Mr. Brown, the PR manager at the Northgate Shopping Center, a very interesting question that I actually had to excuse myself from the meeting and think about before I answered."

Jin's nod confirmed he was listening. He was tired, but it was still at least within his faculties to take in the gist of the conversation.

"Mr. Brown, you see, was pleased that I would take things so seriously, and we arranged to meet again in the afternoon. If I could come up with a reasonable answer, I would get the job for the entire NSC!" Then Uncle D said to his son, "Go left here on Bath Street, please, Art. We'll swing past the NSC so that Jin knows how big an offer this really was!"

Art casually swung the car around to go past the Northgate Shopping Center. Art would have to wait to catch up with Jin on all that had happened and all that was to happen. His load of patience was made lighter by the fact that he needed to concentrate on the road as much as possible in Seattle's city center.

Uncle D continued. "I went down to the market ... oh, we're past that now. I'll take you there sometime soon. Anyway, I went down to the market to clear my head and think about Mr. Brown's question. And do you know what Mr. Brown's question was?"

A small sigh showed that Art had heard the story before, most likely more than once, but Jin's nod indicated that he was willing to find out.

"Mr. Brown asked me, 'How much will it cost my company to get a customer into our shopping center, and what are you going to do to get that cost down?' So I went down to the market and sat in front of the fish market, with my notebook and a cup of yogurt to keep me company. It took time. I was determined not to go away from my spot until I had an answer. Much time went by, and I still had no answer to Mr. Brown's question. All this time was going by while I was 'entertained' by the workers at the fish market.

"It was only after I opened my eyes to it that I learned the principles of being 'world famous' and discovered my answer. Ultimately, I was influenced to make a rather rash decision. It was more a moment of frustration, actually, as best I can recall. I put my neck out on the line."

As they passed the Northgate Shopping Center, it became obvious to Jin just how important a contract this must have been for Uncle D. The center was huge. They must have sold just about everything, as Art mentioned, finally able to get a word in edgeways.

"Eyes on the road, son," was Uncle D's response. It made Art's distraction from the task given short lived.

"Uncle D? You do all their advertising? Your company must be enormous!" Jin looked in awe as the center went on and on, city block after city block.

"Not exactly, Jin. We have eight exclusive contracts with similar shopping centers throughout the state." Jin's jaw dropped. His uncle must be rich! "It's not as flashy as it sounds. We invest 25 percent of our profit margins back into our clients laterally, to ensure that our marketing is more successful than what any other advertising agency can offer. It's been a long and difficult journey to get here,

Jin. Though I prefer the word 'challenging' over 'difficult,' because it has a more positive feeling about it."

They finally passed the center and were on their way home as Uncle D explained more. "There are only two forms of advertising: internal and external. Externally, it is difficult to measure the success of a good or even great advertising campaign. However, it *is* quantifiable. Whatever can be measured can be improved upon. I went back proudly to our meeting at two o'clock and sat with Mr. Brown again. We concurred that were the NSC to do no advertising, there would be a result: people would still attend the center. Chances were that it would be less and less attendance over time, perhaps taking about a year or so to know what that result would be. We could then satisfactorily say that the difference between whatever result that experiment provided and what attendance was present would be the net result of marketing.

"As it was both impractical and implausible to perform such a test, we had to agree that advertising did provide some sort of positive influence on the attendance of potential patrons at the shopping center. Whatever can be measured can be improved upon. We just needed to design a system that was measurable. I suggested that internally, we create a system not only to get patrons in, but to reduce the cost per patron of getting them to return—measurably. It was this unique selling point, or USP, that my company would offer as a service to the NSC for no extra charge, to consistently improve upon our external results no matter how great they may be.

"The NSC now uses a loyalty card system we set up involving points that customers can accumulate and later cash in on. Every customer of that shopping center is voluntarily catalogued and will then receive a thank-you for shopping at NSC. If they return with a colleague within the next fourteen days, they will receive double the points for their colleague's purchase by redeeming a coupon. Those coupons were the measurable difference that my company would provide at no additional fee, and that's why I originally got their advertising contract.

"Everybody sells! Even a secretary who answers the phone at a doctor's office needs to sell an appointment. She may not receive commission, but any secretary who understands her position and performs accordingly is a valuable asset.

"The NSC and I have enjoyed a successful working relationship ever since those days, and Mr. Brown has long since personally referred my company further; landing me two substantial contracts in other cities. Oh, we're here."

Before getting out of the car, Uncle D turned and spoke to both boys. "It is my sincerest wish for each of you to understand things as they really are, and for you to realize that whatever path you find yourself on, you trust it is the right one for you at the moment. This may be a great aspect of personal wisdom and will provide you the inner peace to see things through, to grasp the impermanent and imperfect nature of everything around you.

"But it is not necessarily an intellectual capacity, just as wisdom is not just a matter of intelligence. You will have to utilize the capacities of your minds to attain, sustain, and enhance where you find yourself, no matter where it may be. All beings are subject to suffering; this is the true nature of all things. Since our view of the world forms our thoughts and our actions, having the right view yields right thoughts and right actions."

It was a little late for a lesson in philosophy, but the boys did their best to take in what Uncle D said, because he said it with such conviction. The difficulty of comprehension of his words was apparent to him even as he spoke, so Uncle D turned to lighter themes. "Get some rest, and we'll talk about what you want to do as soon as you're up for it."

A well-rested morning came to Jin, and he had made his way to the kitchen, where he found his uncle already busy preparing for the day. Upon seeing Jin, Uncle D greeted him with the sincerest of hopes that he had enjoyed a good night's sleep, and then he got straight to the point. It was by no means too early for such a conversation today.

"It's wise to go someplace you can seclude yourself, before making a big decision, so you can take your time making it. I would suggest someplace private where you can feel detached from everything else and are able to concentrate on the matter at hand; that way all your energy is moving to bring you the best solution as quickly as possible. It's not so important where you are as much as how open you are for the answer to come to you from your surroundings.

"As you are not from here; I will share with you today where I go. That location may or may not inspire you. I cannot know that—who can? I only know that this place worked for me many, many times. I will bring you there and set you off so that you can have some time to yourself. Then, I must get to the office to work on some marketing."

Jin nodded and stifled a yawn. Although having completed his morning rituals, the jet lag was still playing havoc with his alertness. Breakfast in America was going to take some getting used to. Today was a day he might have envied Art for being allowed to sleep in. Hopefully it wouldn't take long to readjust to the time difference.

After getting a few things loaded into the car for Uncle D, they were on their way. Jin wondered to himself, but he also said it aloud. "What exactly is marketing supposed to do, Uncle? How does it work?"

Uncle D replied, "Well, conventionally, marketing is seen as being just advertising. Luckily for me, most other advertising businesses see it that way as well. I see it as prospecting: it's everything that happens before potential customers enter the business with thoughts about purchasing an item or service. They may not have even heard of your product or service before. I suppose it's safe to say it's the first step in the sales process. You see, the sales process is like a circle: at any given time, you might find yourself at any given point along the sales process. Some people think of the process as a wheel having eight steps. There is always a 'before' and 'after' step, but prospecting is as good a point as any to start."

Jin stared out the car window to take in as much as possible. As they approached Seattle, there was a distinction from the green and rather winding roads that brought one to the city from the seemingly impossible weave of bridges and roads. The city planning may have been something to keep the tourists out. Uncle D made some lane changes that only a local could do comfortably, to get through the thickest street traffic before coming out into a more rural part of the city. The sun was doing its best to poke through the clouds.

Seattle people seemed to walk with their eyes wide open, and they were often engaged in conversation. Old or young couples seemed genuinely happy to be in each other's company. It was a likeable place.

"At my company," Uncle D continued, "we pick up what's weakest after the sale has been made and magnify that with an external campaign. What is very important to me at my business is that we all work very hard at having fun with prospecting. My company is very Gung Ho. Do you understand what I mean, Jin?"

"I think so, yes. Gung ho, as in having a 'go for it' or 'go get 'em' attitude, right?"

"Not exactly, although that's not bad for a loose interpretation of what results from our business philosophy. I don't mean gung ho but Gung Ho," he said with a certain distinction between the two. "Gung Ho is a business philosophy, based on a book by the same name, that I've incorporated into my business to ensure the effectiveness and stability of the people who choose to work there.

It's a very simple, three-step process that we allow into just about any area or business as much as possible, and it has worked very well for us. I seem to remember it being called the way of the squirrel, the beaver, and the goose, to make the whole thing easier to remember. It's a great read, and I wholeheartedly recommend you read it when you make the time.

"Basically, each employee spends his or her time foraging for what's to be done whenever it seems there is a lull. That way we have no seasonal downtimes. When there is something to be done, not only do we get to it, but we allow it to be done as it gets done, and we trust that it will be accomplished efficiently. That way we don't repeat the work of others unnecessarily. Lastly, we cheer each other on as much as possible, as a positive reinforcement tool; that way employees are constantly motivated to do things better than they've ever been done before. Ah, we're just about here. Isn't it great?"

Their drive along Alaskan Way provided ample places to park at this hour in the morning. Uncle D and Jin left the security of the parking lot to visit the park and go briefly down to the sea line before heading over to Pike Street. A breeze sharper than any Jin could remember gusted but was not in any way unpleasant. Uncle D and Jin continued to talk as the sea's spray refreshed and awakened their senses, a welcome wake-up call in this new foreign land.

Focus and Punctuality
White Belt

Three Rules of Concentration

- Focus with your eyes.

- Focus with your mind.

- Focus with your body.

Jin inhaled deeply and allowed the fresh sea air to permeate his nostrils. The salt in the air seemed to go right into his very being and get all the kinks out. It made him warmer from the inside by having his heart work harder to push the blood around. The salt-permeated blood traveling through Jin's capillaries even seemed to make his fingertips swell with warmth. It gave him the impression that the people who lived here worked an honest day for an honest day's pay.

Moving further toward some benches allowed the sea's mist to waft its salty scent across the boardwalk enough to remind them where they were: the land of opportunity.

Uncle D directed Jin briefly through town to a particular bench with a clear view of the Pike Place Market. Although America had a limited history, when compared to Asian or European, it managed to establish an antiquity with its marketplaces. Pike Place was no exception. Here was America; here it was kept alive. "Here, Jin, take a seat and think on your martial arts training. What was it Sensei used to say about focusing?"

Jin's fond memories of his martial arts training flooded back quicker than the sound of the next wave rolling into the breakers. Uncle D was an accomplished martial artist and had even taught him before moving to America when his regular instructor, Sensei Iura, was unavailable. Jin smiled, giving back the answer he was required to respond to hundreds of times in class, "Focus with your eyes, focus with your mind, and focus with your body."

Uncle D grinned at the loyalty and correctness of the response with a sense of rekindled pride. "Good. Now, come with me to the Pike Place Fish Market. If you apply those techniques Sensei taught you here, I am confident that you will find the answer to whatever it is that you may be seeking. It will at least allow you to discover the question. I hope the answer comes to you soon, Aramaki-San."

It was a strange truth, but it always made Jin feel good to be addressed formally as "Mr. Aramaki" by his uncle. Now, he was indeed approaching an age where he would be addressed more and more as an adult.

"I will call a colleague of mine this afternoon and see if he knows anyone who has some work available. It won't matter what you do, son; it'll just be something to do until you know more about what it is you really want to do. The right attitude does not go unnoticed, and these guys know something about the right attitude."

Uncle D handed Jin a paper with some bus routes and directions on how to get home, mentioning that it would take about forty minutes to get there. Jin thanked his Uncle for everything he had done and was doing for him. After professing that it was no effort and he was glad to do it for his favorite nephew, Uncle D was on his way back to the car park. Jin took comfort that a new routine might be closer than he thought, and he trusted that his uncle was right. It wouldn't matter what he did; anything was better than nothing, to get his mind off the things that were troubling him of late.

It didn't take Jin long to realize the most dominant detail about the world-famous Pike Fish Market employees: these guys were nuts! Giant catches of seafood were flying in every direction. They were throwing these huge fish around to each other and catching them, yelling and repeating each other for the orders made and where the orders were going.

Finely dressed customers were sometimes throwing fish, if not catching fish. All the while there was a childlike energy about their stand, and no one seemed to mind the grime. Even the sternest looking of people would end up smiling, and the timid usually ended up hysterically laughing. There had to be a reason for it, and Jin was intrigued to learn more of the why.

Jin watched closer as it became apparent that the men were working hard at having fun. The fish market was hard work, of that there could be no doubt. Yet even with all the physical stress, they remained present for every customer. They chose to ignore the environment they found themselves in and to make each person's day as best they could. What's more, the business they were generating was by far dominating the other fishmongers. Jin learned that it didn't matter what he chose to do; as long as he held a passion about whatever it was that he was doing, he would have success doing it.

He went up to thank them for what he had learned and shook hands with one of the guys. It was the wettest, slimiest, fishiest handshake he was glad to ever have received. Jin was genuinely inspired to get a job no matter what the work would be. He took the directions Uncle D had given him and made his way home. He would have to wait to share his conclusions and gratitude with his uncle.

"Uncle," Jin exclaimed upon Uncle D's return from the office, "I would very much like to work as soon as possible. It doesn't matter in what. Is there any way you can help me find some work?"

Uncle D nodded and explained how he had already called a colleague of his at the NSC who needed someone urgently, because the center's hygiene had recently become a concern. "Everyone knows someone who needs something," Uncle D said for the benefit of both boys. "Tell enough people you are seeking work, and you will never be without it. It's just a matter of matching one person's desires with another's."

Jin was glad to get the cleaning job because there was a challenge in improving the general cleanliness and hygiene of the NSC, and it meant an opportunity to get noticed. Art was pleased Jin was focusing on something so positively, and he was sure Jin's attitude would be the one to get noticed.

Uncle D had made the arrangements, and the job was relatively low on the corporate ladder, so there would be no need for an interview. Uncle D mentioned to Jin that it would be a while before he properly knew how to sell himself to a potential employer, and that this was for the time being the best solution. Uncle D assured Jin that the time would come when he wouldn't have to go for an interview because he would become a black-belt salesperson, just as he had become a black-belt martial artist. "The time will come when you will create your own opportunities and take advantage of them, Jin. Not to worry." He placed his hand on Art's shoulder as he continued. "My son has become quite successful at it, a fact of which I am very proud."

Art's humbled demeanor spoke volumes.

It took about a week to get to know the job, and another to know the rest of the team at the NSC. There was a janitorial meeting every Monday morning to catch up on any news, including Jin's arrival. Most were glad there was a new recruit because it meant the workload could be spread out over more people.

It wasn't very often that Art was home. Jin didn't have the opportunity to visit him much, and he wasn't sure when they'd see each other again.

One lazy Sunday morning found each of the boys easing into a late breakfast. Personalized by individual taste, the only thing they shared in common with their brunch was the TV channel: cartoons. The box was simply turned on so that they could tune out, a bit of background noise so that no stressing conversations needed to take place. The volume was low enough so as not to wake Uncle D, and it allowed the two of them to have a serious catch-up conversation.

"It's great seeing you again," Jin opened up.

"You too," Art said in between mouthfuls of cereal. "You look good. Keeping fit, I see."

"Gran's house rules. You remember." Both boys smiled.

"Dad's really pleased with you. He's never been easy to please. How did you manage that?"

Before answering, Jin finished up the fruit he'd set aside for his breakfast, brought their used plates into the kitchen, and popped them into the dishwasher. After returning to the comfort of his coffee and Art's of his Pepsi, the conversation continued. "I never really thought of it, really," Jin replied.

Art said, "All I've been able to figure out is that people are the same wherever you go. We all respond to 'the question.' The most powerful tool I have is my voice, and the most leading way I can get anyone to go in a direction to where I want them to go to is by asking questions. Of course, they have to be the *right* questions … It's like I can control the conversation."

"What if they don't answer?"

"It's very difficult *not* to answer a question, isn't it?"

Jin nodded.

"You see?" Art pointed out. "You nodded. It actually is very awkward not to answer a question. Here, I'll show you. I'll ask you a question, and you try not to answer, and we'll see what happens, okay?"

Jin nodded at the challenge.

Looking about them, Art paused in order to give Jin a chance to prepare himself before asking, "Y'know, I don't know how you can drink that stuff. What do you put in there, anyway?"

Jin bit the urge to respond at Art's comment on his coffee; a silence rose up between the two of them.

"You see?" Art continued. "It kills a conversation not to answer someone. Just as it's possible to carry on or lengthen a conversation by asking more questions."

"Huh." Jin considered Art's words before wondering, "Why do you suppose that is?"

Art shrugged his shoulders while he considered Jin's query. He followed the characters on the tube up until the next punch line before delivering his retort. "I suppose it's because we're human. We all have parents or guardians who looked after us. We were all born—none of us were hatched or cloned to become what we are today. At one point, we were helpless little babies who could do nothing more than cry when something was up. Most likely, some adult figure would say something like, 'Aw, are you tired? Are you hungry? Are you wet?' Eventually some form of communication was developed where we could say what was bothering us, and so we learned how to feel better, or how to say what was bothering us so that someone else would make it go away."

Art and Jin slouched into the couch and let the cartoon end as they enjoyed each other's company.

"All I do is ask questions," Art added. "A lot of questions. If I'm in doubt, I ask. If I have no doubts, I ask." Jin nodded in understanding.

"Being in control of a conversation means being the one asking the questions. Being in control doesn't mean being an ass.

"I do my best at remaining personable, of course; I'm never forceful. If people ask a question, and I don't know the answer, I'll tell them that I don't know but can find out for them, if they'd like to know. If they ask a question I don't want to answer, I might ask them why they want to know that, or whether it's that important for them to know. The truth is, anyone can ask for whatever he or she wants. Without asking, you're guaranteed not to receive whatever it is that you want."

It was a great afternoon spent reconnecting with one another. With the direction their schedules were about to go, it would be some time before they'd have the opportunity to do so again.

Consistency and Effort
Purple Belt

The Four Areas of Mental Focus

- Rate yourself on a scale from one to ten.
- Am I the sharpest in the class?
- Is it real?
- Am I improving?

The crew at the NSC may have been hard working, but they were far from the top in terms of their effectiveness. The reality of the situation was that the shopping center was clean. There could be no arguing the hygiene of the center. To be the sharpest cleaning team in Seattle meant they would have to improve somehow, but how?

One Monday morning, Jin remembered Gran's wise words on being completely dressed, and his consistent smiling became the topic of discussion. One of the other employees, who was also not long in America, asked the rest of the group, "You always have smile on your face. Why?"

Fahid's English may not have been strong, but his depth of character made up for it. Fahid spoke for most of the cleaners, not just because his English was generally better than the others, or because he stood a head and one half taller than them, or because he weighed about as much as two of the others; but because he was a man of his word. Jin thought it unfortunate his accent was so strong as to let others see that he was an honest man. Fahid genuinely wanted to know.

Jin articulated as best he could so that not only Fahid but all could understand as best possible. "We may very well be one of the first workers that potential customers have contact with when they enter the center. Our work, the hygienic conditions we produce for the customer, most certainly is. Think about a store that, as you entered it, was dirty and grimy. Would you be likely to make your purchase there? What if the cleaner scowled at you or looked miserable—how would that make you feel?

"Now, imagine another store just next door that was hygienic, and the cleaning person greeted you warmly. Which store would you prefer to enter? Which would you be more likely to return to, regardless of whether you had made a purchase that day?"

Fahid replied, "I like when people nice to me. I go there. Here, I not have good English, though. Why me speak when know this? What me say? I be Saudi immigrant … no can change people to buy."

"Our role is key in influencing potential customers within moments of their entrance, more so than our language abilities. If the language is challenging; a smile may suffice. If you are concerned about your confidence in the English language, take action and do something about it. Arrange a study group here at the center, or go to an existing one with other colleagues, to help better their skills as well. A customer's purchase ultimately becomes our paycheck. I want to insure that there is enough for that paycheck each month as much as possible. Don't you?"

"Yes, why not? Is good for me, is good for all peoples."

"And what about the future of our employment? NSC is just a company name; it makes no difference on a résumé whether the NSC was a shopping center or a seniors center, as long as the job was done professionally. That's expected, but it's our attitude that people refer. The quality of hygiene at the NSC should be at the highest standard possible, and we should pride ourselves in that. There's nothing holding this team from being the best team in the city, except ourselves. It starts with each of us doing just one thing, anything, to improve ourselves. My gran used to say to me, 'Believe you can or believe you can't; either way, you'll be right!'"

"We just cleaners. Not managers," Fahid noted.

"Well, if a job title is the only thing holding us back, why don't we change it, for no one else but for ourselves? Perhaps the title could be altered to alter our opinions? What title works for you, Fahid?"

Fahid turned to his colleagues, and the conversation that ensued assured them that "manager'" was too lowly a position. If they truly were to choose a title for themselves, it needed something with more clout, something in which each person would take pride. They finally settled on hygienic engineers.

"Right, I like it. That's good! Now, it's up to each one of us to define what a hygienic engineer is. What can we do differently to get the recognition of that title?"

They drew up a list of the things they didn't like, as well as what responsibilities they could actively take to eliminate those negative things. Additionally, the blue engineers' team would make themselves noticed to the public in as positive a way as they could manage. Everyone was involved, like a military operation where none would be left behind. Each was left to play his or her part to the best of his or her ability, and then they praised him or her as often as possible.

The same work continued but was now charged with more enthusiasm. The weekly meetings became all about sharing what each person had done and celebrating that accomplishment, no matter how seemingly insignificant. More conversations meant the employees exercised more language skills, and Jin was astonished at the rate of improvement that made. They made themselves seen! The heavy blue overall uniforms were now coming in pressed and cleaned. Everyone bragged about how many people they had managed to assist that day and that week, even if it was by brightening people's day with a warm smile.

Jin was pleasantly surprised to be greeted with a heartfelt "Nice to see you, Jin. You're looking well today!" The greeting came from Rashid and an elderly gentleman whom he hadn't yet met. Both men had escaped from horrors in Herzegovina. Though an accent was there, the illusionary threat of Rashid's obvious, if not ominous, foreignness was set aside by the sincerity in his greeting.

"Language barriers are there for what purpose, students?" Jin could hear his old English teacher, Mr. Wil, speaking that rhetoric: "They are little more than opportunities. They provide us an opportunity to expand our listening skills, which you will find very important in life, Mr. Aramaki. But additionally, and perhaps even more beneficial to us as a race, is that learning another person's language allows for greater understanding of cultural barriers."

Jin had fond memories of Mr. Wil's firm but fair manner of teaching. There was always a large mug of seemingly never-ending coffee on his desk, which the teacher took great pleasure in sipping as the lesson rolled on. Mr. Wil had formerly been the athletic coach at the school until age had caught up to him and the politics of school life became boring; then he sat as a grand figure behind the desk in Jin's past. He had influenced Jin to be intrigued by English and to learn it to the best of his ability. It was Mr. Wil's suggestion that he try the advanced literature course, if he was having such difficulties grasping the subtleties of English.

"Why would I want to do poorly in *two* classes, Mr. Wil?" Jin had complained.

"Not at all, Jin. The two courses complement each other and will enhance your comprehension threefold. Poetry, writing, and song—all are art, any one of which arguably might very well be language's highest form of expression. But how can we hope to understand the artists if we cannot put into context what they are saying?"

Upon graduation Jin had received an award in English. Not bad for a country kid who had not known a word of English five years prior to that.

Unbeknownst to Jin was what had gone on behind his back at the NSC. It was weeks later that Jin got called into the office to find out what it was. Mr. Brown's secretary had mentioned that her boss wanted to speak to Jin personally. *It must be serious,* he thought as the secretary asked him to wait with a sort of compassion in her voice that in some way implied, "Sorry to see you go."

Even though her words claimed, "Mr. Brown will see you now," the softness in her tone hinted, "You seem like a nice enough kid ... too bad." It was perhaps the way she carefully placed the receiver down that gave away she must have just been in a private conversation with the boss.

After inviting Jin to sit, Mr. Brown looked at Jin from across his desk, and he edged a pile of paperwork toward Jin. "Who's idea was this, son?" Mr. Brown allowed a pause for retort and gave his undivided attention. Mr. Brown was a modest-looking man. As best Jin could tell, he was about the same age as Jin's uncle. It was difficult to tell because guessing someone's age was often difficult when dealing with people of different ethnic backgrounds. He seemed genuinely interested to learn what had happened.

Jin took careful note of the papers in front of him. There were numbers all over with figures of dollars and cents. Some were underlined, others were circled in red, and still more had red notes with lots of question marks. Jin couldn't make much out of it other than it had to do with money. Company money.

Mr. Brown explained that a course in the staff room for employees meaning to better their English skills was being offered for free. The course had soon outgrown the conference room's capacity. Due to demand, the course now broadened its scope to include family members and even colleagues of staff. It would appear charging money for the ongoing course didn't deter from people enrolling. The course was now earning money and had just graduated its first student, Fahid Amil.

No wonder that the team's English was improving, and that Fahid's accent had diminished so readily! This news explained how some of the team were able to greet people, let alone give directions and advice if necessary.

"Fahid says this is your idea. Is that true?"

"The suggestion was mine, but I would imagine Fahid must have taken it to heart and organized the whole thing."

"Why did you suggest it?"

"I was taught that every cog in a business can be improved upon. My uncle taught me the principles of Gung Ho and took me to Pike Place Fish Market to show me that these principles could be applied under any circumstances. I only meant to put forward those ideals to the rest of my colleagues. It was just an idea off the top of my head! I humbly apologize if I have insulted anyone for overstepping my bounds."

Mr. Brown's hands dropped. "Apologize? Complaints are down. Customers are returning with greater frequency and spending more on average. Profits are up because of something 'off the top of your head,' and you mean to apologize?"

Jin was somewhat dumbfounded by the way the conversation was going.

"Son, this gang-ho fish-thingy idea of yours now pays the cleaning products bill. I've decided to get all new uniforms for the team as well as lessen the load for each of them by hiring more staff. We'll pull the next five eligible graduates from the course for job interviews and hire three of them as a reward for finishing the course. I want you to break the good news to Fahid. Oh, and tell him he's promoted. I want him to manage this gang-ho thing of yours."

"Yes, sir." Jin shuffled in his chair, preparing to leave. "Er, right away, sir."

"As for you, son, I'd like you to think about entering our sales team. I'm curious what you can do with them. Training starts Monday. Normally, it'd be Mr. Page who would be training you, but he's on holiday, so it'll be Ms. Gardner who will get your training started. It'll mean a pay raise, plus commissions. What d'ya say, son?"

Perhaps a job in sales was the next best place for Jin to grow.

Goal Setting
Yellow Belt

The Black-Belt Success Cycle

- Know what you want.
- Have a plan.
- Get a good success coach.
- Take consistent action.
- Review your progress and reset your goals.

Fahid's family was pleased with the news and invited Jin for dinner on the weekend. They ate an Arabic meal in a traditional fashion, with each person reaching to eat together from one central plate. Fahid showed genuine gratitude for the idea that had landed him the new position and a pay increase. The experience was made more bountiful by the kindredness and gentleness of Fahid's family.

Fahid's beautiful wife, Nedja, was a tiny little thing, made to appear even more so next to Fahid's mass of character—yet she ran the house, of that there was no doubt. In broken English, she told Jin how he would always be welcome in their home, and their two children gave Jin enormous hugs of thanks for all he had done.

To Jin, it seemed such a small thing. He thought it amazing that when applied correctly, what a difference a thing of seemingly no particular consequence could make for so many.

The same successfully applied idea got Jin to his meeting on Monday morning.

Jin showed up Monday morning hoping for the best but having prepared for the worst. Ms. Birgit Gardner stood in front of those attending to lead the meeting.

All Jin was able to assess from the other sales people in the conference room was that Birgit Gardner had a notoriously fierce reputation as a woman who didn't fear tearing egos apart, even publicly, if challenged. A conservative suit hugged a rather sturdy figure just enough to squeeze all the right bits out without leaving her overexposed. Square-rimmed glasses would've made a rather hard image, were it not for the green eyes behind them that lightened the overall image even from a distance.

Jin was not surprised to see the sales-training lioness so well prepared. More unexpected was observing her reaction to seeing the group in front of her. They expected a roar, but Ms. Gardner smiled and filled the room with an unexpected charm. "Good morning, and thank you for coming. My name is Ms. Gardner; please call me Biggi. I dearly appreciate you all making the effort this morning, as it is due to my flight later this afternoon that we've all had to meet so early. Believe me, six o'clock doesn't feel any less early whether you are attending or presenting. Let's all make the decision together to be here as participants and take it from there. We'll see what happens."

Biggi had a cheerful tone that took the dread out of the morning. She seemed a likeable combination of firm and fair. "Introducing yourself is an art. Everything we do in life can be seen as an art." She waved her hand toward Jin in a way that made him feel both acknowledged and valued as she continued. "Good friends like those from our neighboring Japan have shown this idea in their culture centuries ago. This training, of which I hope to successfully play my role with those of you here today, is to teach you the first steps in the art of selling.

"The first acknowledgment, then, is that everybody sells. We all do it, each and every one of us. Those who say they don't simply aren't aware of what it is that they sell. The trouble is that when asked who would you trust most, a doctor or a salesperson—or who you'd most like to meet and even date—salespeople unfortunately have a stereotype about them. Whenever most people think of a salesperson, they're thinking of some greasy, unlikeable, shady character, and perhaps even a derelict of a person who's out to rip them off. Whose word is it that we accept with little or no objection? Who comes to mind when you think of the most trustable person within the community outside of family?"

"I trust my doctor." That one response was audible just above the other murmurings across the table.

"Exactly," Ms. Gardner said. "Truth be known, doctors do little more than sell us medicine and surgeries these days; there are just as many unscrupulous doctors as there are salespeople. In any field this is true … so we're all simply people. No surprises there then, are there?

"So I'm inviting you to forget about that imagery and create your own. Be yourself and simply become more aware. Accept this truth and get comfortable with it. Acceptance will, in turn, be the beginnings of creating a great salesperson. Now, let's get started, as I'm afraid I haven't as much time with you as I'd like. As I said earlier, I've been called in on short notice to cover for Steven, and I'm flying out of town later this afternoon."

Uneasiness crept into Jin. Although it had been months, the thought of flying wasn't appealing at all. He could feel his feet pressing into the floor and heard a distant squeal ringing through his memories as Birgit continued. "I'm to visit my husband at his restaurant, which has just been nominated for the prestigious J. Oliver Award. The restaurant is well respected by those in the industry for the quality of food it represents. Organically grown Argentinean beef that is presented alongside freshly boiled, sea-salted, and rosemary-garnished red potatoes from Prince Edward Island in Canada—it's the best cultural dish of the Americas. So, I'm going to talk about cooking for a while."

Upon seeing the heads turn from the desks questioningly, she continued. "Now that I have your undivided attention, please allow me to continue. Not the Shake 'n Bake kind of cooking, but cooking with passion. Cooking with passion translates to selling with passion, and vice versa. This is the bridge I'm going to use to accelerate your learning curve. My husband is a chef, and one of the specialties of his restaurant is steak. The quality of steak purchased at my husband's restaurant is very high, and each piece is to be cooked and served with pride. Each worker there realizes the importance of his or her work, knowing that it is worthwhile.

"I'm sure all of you can cook one thing or another quite well. To be fair to everyone, we're going to talk about cooking steak. So make a note on the top of your paper, on a scale from one to ten: How well can I cook a steak to someone else's liking? Now, we all have our own beliefs about ourselves, so some of you may have chosen a number slightly lower or slightly higher than your actual ability to cook a steak, but we're not going to worry about that for now.

"Steak, as you know, is prepared in three basic varieties: medium, well done, and rare. Not in that order, by the way, but you all know what I'm talking about. When you're learning how to cook steak, it needs to be tested, and the only way to do that correctly is by touch. The tenderness of the meat tells us how cooked the steak is. Chefs have known about this for centuries—go figure!" The smile genuinely crept out from the side of Ms. Gardner's mouth as she added, "Still, if organizations want to give awards and fly people all over the place at their expense to people who are especially sensitive to this fact, then who am I to argue?"

Birgit moved to a position at the front of the room where she was sure each person could get a good view. She held her hands out lightly. "Each of you, feel the fleshy bit of your hand between your thumb and forefinger. Okay, now pinch the skin fold there … the bit furthest away from your hand, but not too hard; we're going to call this rare. Next, move your pinching fingers ever so slightly into your hand and lightly pinch the next, fleshier bit. Notice how it's still squishy but firmer than the skin fold? We're going to call this medium. Finally, gently squeeze the slightly firmer bit just a little further in. Let's call that bit well done."

Jin could feel three differing levels of squishiness in his hand. Odd that he'd never noticed before. Why would he, though? He'd had no cause to. Still, there they were. Every team member gathered around, squishing the fleshy bit in between their thumbs and forefingers.

What a sight they were. All heads nodded meekly at Birgit's strange new revelation about their extremities. It was almost as odd as why they continued to talk as Birgit said, "Chefs. You see, ladies and gentlemen, chefs need to test the tenderness of steaks and how they are cooked for their customers, without cutting the steak open to sneak a peek inside. That's reserved for the customer. A finely tuned sense is required for the most meager of tasks in order to create an experience that will ultimately affect their overall experience in the most positive of ways. I'd like you all to turn to the person on your right; you two on the ends, go together. Right, now I'd like each of you to talk about one positive and one negative experience at a restaurant regarding the quality of the food you were served."

Jin talked about his handshake with the monger at the fish market. The immediate irony, of course, was the general "disgustingness" of the fishmonger's hand versus the not caring about the grime. It was both a positive and negative experience. It had come to light that it was the sincerity of a handshake that made the difference.

Mark, the person on Jin's right, agreed that their friends had good handshakes; neither of them could think of a good friend who didn't.

Birgit followed up with another prompt. "What kind of handshakes do we like? Take a moment now to discuss with the person on your left; this time you two on the other end go together and talk about how that affected your relationship with that person."

On Jin's left, Rick and Jin both enjoyed a good handshake, although neither of them could define what made up one. It was easier to talk about the ones they didn't like. Jin's pet peeve was the weak and sloppy handshake, when people laid their fingers in his palm. Rick's dislike was reserved for the knuckle-busters.

It surprised Jin that this was Rick's pet peeve. Rick was extra sturdy, and the hopes of busting Rick's knuckles were certainly hopeless, because Rick had turned wrenches on oil rigs in the prairies for years, and he could easily enough crush back if so provoked. Rick explained, "People think just 'cause I look strong, they have to try this macho stuff on with me, an' that ain't fair. All I want is a good handshake, like anyone else wants. Not wishy-washy but fair. Firm, but fair."

Again, neither Jin nor Rick could remember a good friend who didn't have a good handshake. It seemed as if people with poor handshakes were often forgotten, glanced over, and fell by the wayside—or as Rick hoped, they met up with someone with an equally useless handshake and gave up trying to shake someone's hand ever again.

Birgit concurred, "Truth be told, it's very rarely that we have friendships with people who don't give an appropriate greeting. Few people enjoy a handshake that isn't engaging. What are some things that make a handshake an engaging one?"

Answers ranged from "It depends on who's hand I'm shaking" to "That people smile; that they look you in the eye; that they don't keep holding on; that their hands are clean; that their hands aren't sweaty." One response pricked Jin's ears, and he had to think twice to know if he'd heard what was said correctly: "That they don't try to tickle the palm of your hand while shaking."

Seriously? Jin thought. *There are people who do that?*

Ms. Gardner raised an eyebrow to the likelihood of that person shaking hands with everyone in that manner, and then she requested everyone to take up a new place at the table, "So, why do we shake hands? We certainly didn't always shake hands; the curtsy and bow were around long before. What changed in our society that we suddenly decided to grasp one another's hands? Anyone care to comment on the historical origins of the handshake?"

When no one volunteered to guess, Birgit provided the history. "There are many points contributing to the development of the handshake. The beginnings of the handshake go back to prehistoric times, when strangers met while hunting. Hunters would show an outstretched open hand with no weapon and then proceed past one another from there.[3] Neither party would raise their weapon against the other or cheat one out of the prize game that in those

---

3 http://www.templestudy.com/2008/02/07/the-origin-of-the-common-handshake/. Appendix C: The Origin of the Common Handshake.

times may have meant survival. The outstretched open hand has long been established as a symbol of meaning no ill will.

"Sales are considered by many—in particular, by prospective purchasers—to be a sort of battle. It's not so much a direct confrontation but a sort of collision of wills that will have people cheated out of something if they don't remain on their guard. No one likes thinking he or she is going to be cheated, and so it is that salespeople have gotten a bad rap. A stereotypical greasy car salesman image comes to mind for most when they are asked to describe what a salesperson looks like.

"A sign of not raising a weapon against another is a way of stating that no harm is meant toward them. A proper handshake can be one way of putting a potential customer at ease, by communicating that we mean them no ill will; we are not here to beat them or snatch their kill from them."

Some raised eyebrows and jeers provided a backdrop to the comment.

"In Kenyan etiquette,[4] grasping the right wrist with the left hand while shaking hands demonstrates respect when greeting an elder or someone of higher status. Various tribes are known to have developed their own individual ritual handshakes as signs of agreement or trust. There are still tribes that will place their hands on another person's chest while talking to them as if saying, 'You have my undivided attention.'

"In the Wild West, paper was often tedious to get hold of, let alone being able to draw up agreement details on it. The North American Indians would seal in blood agreements between tribes who didn't know each other as well. Even common tribesmen would strengthen the connections between individuals and commit to each other this

---

4   http://www.kwintessential.co.uk/resources/global-etiquette/kenya.html. Appendix C: Etiquette and Custom in Kenya.

way. It was no light thing to be brothers in blood; it was a common understanding that two people of one bloodline would never do anything purposefully to dishonor their own line.

"At the time, the slitting of palms seemed a bit extreme to the settlers, due to the number of agreements being made. A compromise had to be reached. A bit of spit, considered a rightful and legal exchange of bodily fluids, and the phrase 'My word is my bond' became common understanding. Deals could be made a lot smoother and without the risks of either becoming anemic, or bleeding to death.

There's an idea, and not a bad one, really. Politicians would do well to adopt a similar system for all the agreements they make. There would certainly be a lot more caution about what was agreed to, as well as prioritizing what really needed to be agreed to, and with whom. While we're at it, why don't we let the leaders of the country simply duke it out instead of sending thousands off to war? That would certainly cut our country's budget."

A cheerful Southern man who spoke out loud and clear, "Heck, y'all, Ah'd pay to see that on TV!"

After the laughter died down enough to rise over additional contributions regarding how the country could afford to send countrymen over there to watch the fight for less money, and queries on what the president would wear for the event, Birgit was able to continue. "As a species, no other is as sensitive to the sense of touch as human beings are. We don't even have to touch each other; we can touch ourselves to create emotion in other people. If I lay my hand on my heart like so, it's as if you can feel your hand on your own heart, and I gain a little bit of your trust."

First Impressions

Shaking

Birgit said, "There is no second chance to make a first impression. We are going to set some ground rules to ensure our success at the most positive handshake possible. First, that little squishy bit that we've been talking about is what we're going to use as a grip gauge. We're going to connect our squishy bits together in the handshake."

As the Southerner in the group drew breath to comment, Ms. Gardner darted a look that stopped him in his tracks. "Let's keep the conversation on an adult level here, Mr. Gregory."

"Yes, ma'am," the Southerner said as he backed down from the confrontation; he gave the impression of a kid being caught with his hand in the cookie jar.

Ms. Gardner continued. "In a moment we'll shake hands with two people we haven't yet shaken hands with, and we'll introduce ourselves. We all enjoy handshakes more similar to our own, so we're going to mirror and match our partner's. Off you go. Meet two more people that you haven't shaken hands with. No matter how firm the handshake you receive—let's not go above well done—focus on engaging the person's handshake for the same amount of time that we sense in our partner's hand. You'll feel their hand relax. When you feel them release, release. Smile, and then look them in the eye and introduce yourself."

The exercise proved useful to Jin because it enlightened his awareness. It gave ritual to what was previously taken for granted. In order to be successful, it was necessary to do what successful people did. Shaking a person's hand well was one of those things.

After a few minutes, Birgit said, "Okay, people. We now have a system that will aid us in making the best first impressions. Any questions?"

Mr. Scheers from accounting spoke out. All in the group were made aware of his name because he was the only one at the meeting with a giant name badge with "Hello, my name is …" on it. Underneath, he had neatly filled in "Mr. Scheers" with a line below reading "Accountancy, MA." He spoke as neatly as the pressed suit jacket that now rested on the back of his chair. "What if they've got a lazy eye? Where do you look then? I mean, uh, which eye?"

"Good question. My answer would be not to look in either, but to look at the bridge of the nose. It tends to put people at ease, as opposed to you moving around the room as you try to follow where one eye or the other is looking. Any other questions? No? Good. Okay, we must accept that not everybody will be as aware of their own behavior and what defines a good handshake as you, now that we've had this meeting. The unfortunate truth to the expanding of our consciousness is that the more conscious we are about things, the more conscious we will be of the failings in others. It may annoy us, even eat away at us. Remember that the world needs diversity; smile at their innocence."

After checking her watch, Ms. Gardner gathered her notes. "Oh nuts—the time! I really must be going. The rest of your training will continue, although I'm not actually sure how, as I was doing Mr. Page a favor this morning. Chin up, and good luck!" With that, she left and was on her way to the airport.

But for Jin, upon hearing the word "airport," there was a soaring unease …

Commitment
Orange Belt

The Principles of a Black Belt

- Courtesy
- Humility
- Integrity
- Perseverance
- Self-Control
- Indomitable Spirit

The morning ritual training was on its way when Jin began a sequence of introspection. At around sit-up number fifty, Jin viewed carefully how he meant to increase his knowledge about sales. An increase in knowledge of any sort was a path to improvement. Assured that Uncle D would agree with his cognitive wisdom, Jin volunteered his energy forth with severe intention. A short pause between sets allowed him to assume the position as he mentally prepared for the 150 push-ups he was about to do …

Thanks to Gran's influence, Jin was the type of person who committed himself to improve both ethically as well as mentally. At present he could feel the mental challenge of stepping back on an airplane. He wasn't going to allow his feelings of aversion toward flying get in the way of his self-improvement.

Jin's breathing established a regular pattern as his view shifted to see how a balance was established with one force pulling at him to learn all he could, and another suppressing his willingness to get anywhere. This was unacceptable, and change was inevitable.

As the morning's push-ups became more challenging, remnants of aggression and anger left Jin's person. Now fully awake and focused, Jin's sense of self-compassion developed toward his present predicament.

I know what I want, he thought to himself. *An opportunity has presented itself; so I'm going to go for it.*

And Jin's day began harmlessly enough ...

Courage and Self-Control
Green Belt

Have you PASSED? That is, have you:

- P – Practiced at *home*?
- A – Had the correct *attitude*?
- S – *Shouted* on all the techniques?
- S – Performed those techniques *sharp* and not sloppy?
- E – Had lots of *energy*?
- D – Shown *dedication* to your training?

With Biggi having flown the coop and Steven still on holiday, the newly trained sales team was left to its own devices. It would have to be on-the-job training from here on in. Each section of the NSC was broken down by department, where one salesperson would responsibly have the floor. The people Jin had trained with were spread out based on necessity and personal interest as best as possible.

Notably, Mr. James Robert Thorton, or Jim-Bob, from whom Jin remembered his Southern wit, was assigned to the rod and gun shop. When customers were unsure what exactly they were looking for in hunting equipment or apparel, expressions like "Lemme help ya git yer trigga-finga on it" worked for Jim-Bob. He was a natural in his element.

Jin was also assigned to the rod and gun sports department. Jin's only source for information for the time being was the existing senior salesperson and floor manager, Mr. Matthias Czeronowsky.

Always meaning to "Get back to you" on whatever the inquiry was but never actually doing so wasn't much help in knowing what to do. Jin felt totally out of his element. Not knowing what else to do, he made the best of it and took to greeting the customers as they came in as best as he could.

It was one of the other salespeople, Miss Steffi Schuld, who was helpful in teaching Jin what needed to be done. She really was a lovely girl. Her instructions came at a tornado pace that left Jin unsure of the third thing that had to be done in the morning for the opening of the "all sports" department. Steffi proved to be an all-around sports enthusiast. If it was sporty, she was either doing it or had tried it. Friendly enough and genuinely interested, Steffi was easily able to encourage visitors to get excited and make their purchases then and there.

Jin was fascinated to hear how Steffi had never seen a real magazine until she was eighteen, because she was from the eastern part of Germany. Sport was Steffi's way of escaping poverty. She had grown up in a family absent of wealth. When the Berlin Wall came down, she wanted out as far as possible. The West greeted the East in a rather unfriendly manner, calling them Össies. It was an unkind combination of the German words for foreigner and easterner. However, she had met someone in Hamburg who treated her with kindness and showed her that it was possible to use the term Össie with the greatest of affection, teaching her that she could use it to empower herself. Even now, nearly on the other side of the globe, the American term for someone from Australia, an Aussie, remained a painful reminder of her childhood and overt heritage.

Though her background in was incredibly diverse, it was obvious she wasn't hired for her knowledge in sports. Living in poverty and performing so much had kept Steffi trim and sinewy. Steffi was most comfortable wearing tight-fitting T-shirts that emphasized the fact that she had breasts, and she didn't mind the attention.

"Sex sells; it's a fact," she'd say whenever reprimanded for customer complaints about how revealing her clothing was on colder days. "The complaints—are they from women or men?" They were always from women. "And these women—are they fit or not?" Usually they were not. "So are they complaining about my noticeable nipples, or that their husbands noticed my nipples?" She'd embarrass the boss into admission, and thereby submission. There she'd be the next day, busting out at the front of the store, and she'd attract a number of people into the store. A few comments here and there about "Where do you train?" or "What are you looking to improve?" would usually cinch the deal.

That being said, the first few days went splendidly. As the week went on, Jin might have capitalized on Steffi's "assets," but it was still his sincerity toward the customer that closed the sale. Jin was meeting daily targets easily enough.

Surprisingly, what was really likeable about Steffi was her kinship toward children and mothers with children. She was always quick to compliment mothers regarding how good they looked, and she'd talk to them about motherhood.

It was only after getting to know Jin enough that Steffi revealed in a tearful manner that she couldn't have children due to her poverty-stricken childhood, which had caused her uterus to prolapse. She was barren and was embarrassed that she had gotten the job solely based on how she looked. Her performance, consistently hitting targets, was overshadowed by a floor manager to whom she'd said no. Now he was in the way of her advancement.

Jin spoke to dozens of people each day. After a while, Jin's sales dropped off a bit. Steffi told Jin not to worry because this happened to everyone. "Besides," she said, "Mr. Page will be back soon and will be able to help you with it."

It seemed that people were entering the store to ask where this or that was in the center. Either Jin knew or he didn't, and he would give appropriate directions when he could.

Though they were still on target, both Steffi and Jin were to receive an unpleasant meeting with the floor manager. Mr. Czeronowsky either didn't accept or didn't care that Jin's efforts were good for the center. Both Jin and Steffi got grilled regarding how many of their customers came to them because of the efforts of other departments giving people directions to the department. Steffi was outright accused of knowing better than to waste time talking to people who weren't the store's customers. The floor manager didn't take too well to Steffi's sarcastic suggestion that they would do so much better to outright ignore every directly asked question from anyone who hadn't yet made a purchase at the store.

After the meeting, Jin felt disheartened and asked Steffi what he was doing wrong.

"Nothing, Jin. Nothing. The only thing going against you is that you have no action plan, and Matthias isn't going to give you one. How can he expect you to get wherever he means for you to get to? Look, the difference is that when you first came here, you were trying everything; it was all so new and so dynamic to you. You tried so many things with each person that something eventually worked. Now you're using the same things that worked for a few people for the majority of others, and that can't be a formula for success. People are different, and we need to identify those differences and capitalize on them.

"I use something called DISC analysis to identify general personality traits in individuals, so I know how to engage them—at least initially. Has Matthias trained you at that?"

"Matthias keeps meaning to train me, but he hasn't had time to do so."

"Oh, bull! Half the time he spends on the phone to his mates regarding how they're going to score this weekend or how they almost did last weekend, and the other half he's on the phone with his wife explaining how he'd never do her wrong."

"That's very sad."

"I'll say! He's a very sad person; I pity him a little, actually. Matthias seems to think he's God's gift to women, and he lives a life of lies and deceit. He'd like everyone to believe that he's a playboy whom all the ladies want. He never gets anywhere with any of them, but he is too ignorant to notice. As long as you play ball with him and go along with whatever he says, you'll get along with him fine. To deny is to defy him, and he doesn't take too kindly to that, to say the least. He'll find something to use against you. Unfortunately, we're answerable to Mr. Czeronowsky, so watch your back, Jin—he'll stick a knife in it when it suits him to do so."

"You really think so?"

"Pick up line three anytime he's on the phone and 'doesn't have time for you,' and make your own opinion. He only hired me 'cause of my tits."

Jin remained focused on her eyes, blinking slowly to control the male's natural glancing reflex upon hearing the reference. "I'm sure they're lovely, but isn't there anyone we can rely on for sound advice and training?"

"Sure. Steven Page. Come on, Jin. Don't let him win. Don't give in to Matthias. Hold on just a little bit longer. You'll see."

"What's he like, this Mr. Page?"

"Steven? He's the man! There's a role model for employees and other men. You follow his example, and you'll do fine. I can train you a little bit about what I remember from Steven's teachings on DISC theory. It's not all that difficult. Once you get that down, you'll be promoted out of here in no time. But when you do get out of here, you have to promise to come back and rescue me. Deal?" Steffi smiled.

"Deal!"

Jin and Steffi shook hands on it, and the running private joke between them was, "When's prison break?" It would always bring a smile to Steffi's face, and when the joke got old, Jin began to refer to their department as Alsportraz, which cemented their professional kinship.

DISC

What Are You?

Understanding DISC analysis[5] was one way of working smarter, as Steffi began explaining to Jin the very next day. "DISC is about generalizing, or about making generalizations about people in order to better know how to deal with them. Basically there are four generalizations, of which any two can be combined to give a main and secondary characteristic for any given individual. Or you can look at it like all people fit into certain patterns.

Jin followed her instruction well. Steffi's description was followed easily enough. "DISC is an acronym for 'dominant, impulsive, secure, and cautious' personality types. No one should ever be thought of as superior to another. Steven is very particular about this point for some reason."

Not recalling exactly why that was so important, Steffi went on to explain the various types. It hadn't been so apparent to Jin before how true DISC was. "Dominant people are those who are very direct. They just want to know the price. Time is always pressing, and they will consistently try to dominate any given conversation. They're usually more formally dressed and would most likely feel most comfortable in a three-piece suit. They're the work-hard-play-hard types. They even tend to walk a certain way: very tunnel-

---

5   Appendix D: DISC Analysis.

visioned and quick paced. Their feet seem to ... well, like that guy there."

Jin turned to where Steffi indicated, and sure enough there was a conservatively dressed businessman whose feet stormed along the floor as he checked his watch twice while sipping his Starbucks coffee. Without breaking pace, he was able to answer his cell phone in the same hand that held a newspaper. It was only as he walked by that Jin was able to hear the gentleman demand from whoever was on the other side of the phone, "Uh hmm. So, how much?"

Whatever answer was given only caused the man to stop briefly in front of a store window, glance inside, check his watch again, and then storm off along the same route on which he'd started. This was not the guy who would be at his best when waiting in a queue.

"D-types want to have people around them know how busy they are and that their time is valuable. It may be that they are starved for recognition. All you have to do to get them to listen is save them the hassle of convincing you of all that. Explain to them how you know that they don't have much time, or how something will save you both a lot of time, and ask direct questions.

"I-types, or impulsive types, make up the majority of all purchasers. They want whatever's new, whatever's in fashion with extra flash, and they want it right away. They tend to want more to gossip than to attempt deep, intellectual conversations. They see things for how pretty they are and do so with a great deal of emotion. You can usually hear them as well as see them."

At that moment a girl approached them on her cell phone. "And so like, oh my god, and it was so totally such a blast, and like, we were all by the pool, and the brother to that girl who knows the cousin of the person who invited me there was like, Mr. Octopus, with arms all over me with me. I was like, 'Whoa, you might be all Mr. Fantastic where you're from, but you smoke, and that is, like, so Mr. Lame-O, y'know?' And then there was this …" There didn't seem to be a breath between acknowledging that there were, in the window beside her, shoes. "Shoes! Oh, like shoes! I totally have to call you back, okay? So like, ciao-ciao for now. Bye, babe." With the click of the phone being closed, she asked Steffi, "How much are like, those shoes in your window? Do you have them in a six? Do you have them in red?"

Steffi waited for the moment to get a word in edgewise before asking a question to the girl, who was already laden with shopping bags from various stores. "What are they for?"

The young girl went into a whirlwind of explanation, of which Jin was only able to make out that she had just bought a red dress and had to find sports shoes to match in color, like another girl had done at a party the week before.

Steffi took the girl around the store to accessorize the sporty-dress look with more authentic color-coordinated pieces. The girl was happily on her way when her cell jingled out the latest Avril Lavigne tune before she shuffled answered. "So like, where is the party this weekend, babe? I have *totally* got the perfect outfit, and there's no way I'm going to let the cousin of that girl who dissed *my* best friend get the attention of that total babe guy from last week that was getting his face sucked by that …" And with that, she was off.

Jin stood flabbergasted at Steffi's successful return. "I-type?" he inquired, half-smirking.

"Oh, yes! Doesn't get much more 'I' than that." They laughed. "Now then, where were we? Oh yes—S-types! Some people seek security. These are the people who despise change above all else. They just need to hear that they are understood—or more appropriately, that *you* really understand their concern, and that it'll be all right. Just tell them, 'I understand,' and they'll buy. I should mention that S-types rarely come out. You can identify them best by the way they tend to peer at things from a distance, often seeming timid.

They're the ones who are generally 'just looking' most of the time. They enjoy the security of things that stay the same; it gives them comfort to know that old values aren't lost. They also want to know that those values are going to be there in the years to come."

The day went on as Jin heard about C-types, otherwise known as the cautious personality type. They made great accountants and statisticians.

Jin recalled his meeting with the accounting department just after being hired, to set up his employee number and bank wiring details. There sat the MA from accounting he had met at Biggi's sales meeting before him, with a pocket calculator complete with a host of integral functions probably powerful enough to chart a course around the sun for the Hubble telescope. With that and a notebook on the table. the person Jin spoke to didn't want to miss a detail.

What was this guy's name, anyway? Damn name tag; it had stopped Jin from feeling the need to remember his name ... Oh well, it didn't matter for now. Jin looked at his attire and demeanor and thought to himself, *I'm no C-type.*

Apparently C-types would have the most amazingly detailed and sometimes unusual questions about a product or service. *Definitely not me,* Jin mentally confided to himself.

Later, Steffi explained, "The only way I know of to identify C-types is that they tend to write really, really long e-mails, and quite regularly. As long as you're well informed about the service or product you are offering, and you can either answer their question or get the answer for them, they'll buy."

Working in sales at the NSC was as varied as the customers that visited it. There were long hours that seemed to go on without end, but other days when the time flew by. That was the way of sales.

A commissioned pay structure meant that if Jin wanted to earn more, he needed to work smarter, not harder. Jin had learned the basic ropes and was still holding on. With every personality type there was both a major and a minor type identifiable. Some types mixed easily, whereas others conflicted. A C-type would have difficulties trying to be a D-type, just as an S-type would have difficulties being spontaneous, or an I-type.

There was no "best" type to be. Jin met nice people in all categories. He did his best to be nice to everyone, and for the most part, people returned it in kind. For those occasional times someone was particularly rude or oddly miserable, he and Steffi would later talk about it privately and find a way to laugh about it. At the end of the day, they had done their best. It was more appropriate to feel sympathetic toward those customers; obviously, those people's behavior was only reflecting some element of themselves with which they were truly unhappy.

"Could you be happy if your partner ran away with the plumber or the neighbor? If you looked like your dog, or if your dog looked better? If your partner ran away with the neighbor's dog?" The steam-releasing sessions (SRSs) designed to crack them up were never taken seriously and usually turned back fairly quickly to typing people they mutually knew.

Ms. Gardner was an ID-type. She had that dominant subtype about her that she could bring out at a moment's notice whenever necessary. Fahid was an SC-type. The stability aspect of his being able to support his family took precedent over his attention to detail and careful planning. His ultimate caution had resulted in the NSC earning money from a resource it didn't even know it had.

Uncle D was a D-type, though it eluded Jin what his subtype was, either S or C. Uncle D wore three-piece suits and felt most comfortable when formally dressed—something Jin's cousin, Art, never aspired to do. Art's meticulousness for ironed slacks and shirts was merely because it had to be done for his job. Art sought security in a business world and in expressing his creativity; he was an SI-type.

Steffi said, "We all express more of our I-type when we're on vacation." It made sense; Jin hadn't met a tourist yet who wasn't an I-type. When people were shopping, there was likely to be more of that I-type spontaneity, but it was not necessarily so.

And Steffi? She was direct and to the point in every way. Most likely she was a double-D type.

Thursdays were promotional sales days, where people who had entered a drawing to win a free month's membership and a training outfit from All Sports came around to collect their prizes. Truth be known, everybody who entered won. Each and every entrant was called the week before with some cheesy radio-announcer-like voice (Mr. Czeronowsky) informing them they were a winner. Entrants could come down and pick up their prize on the coming Thursday between the hours of ten and twelve o'clock. It was never more apparent how innocent contest entrants were of the fact that everyone won as on this day. At five minutes before ten o'clock that morning, Jin heard the cries.

"Oh yeah!" boomed a voice in the mall. "I won! I won, I won!"

Jin turned to see where this powerful voice was coming from and was confronted with the eyes of Mr. Legg. There stood a man head and shoulders above the rest. He was severely overweight and was sweating profusely through his 4XL gray T-shirt. But it wasn't the way this man lumbered—he did lumber along, momentum in motion and all—it was his eyes that caught Jin off guard.

Mr. Lance Legg wore spectacles like none other Jin had seen. The glasses were so convex that the image of Mr. Legg's eyes filled the entire frames.

These prescription fire-starters still did not seem to be powerful enough for him. Amazingly, one could make out that Mr. Legg was squinting from time to time to read signs on shops as his momentum carried him down the mall.

"Where's Al's Sports? Where's the sports store?" He shot out exasperated or exhausted cries in every direction. "I won! Yahoo, I won something!"

Those glasses—for some reason, Jin couldn't keep his eyes off of them! It was as though they refracted light in a way that slowed down time; even blinking took the same amount of time it took to say, "Blink-blink." Jin informed the exasperated man that he was, in fact, at All Sports.

"Wahoo!" the man enthusiastically cried with a double blink.

Still mesmerized by the fact that Hubble hadn't thrown this man in jail for the obvious theft of their replacement lenses, Jin regained his composure enough to introduce himself. "Welcome, my name's Jin. How can I help you today?"

Mr. Legg gasped for breath while answering. "My name … is Lance Legg … and I'm a winner!" Blink-blink. "I ain't never won … nuttin' before, but I sure won this time!" Mr. Legg drew a deep breath before expressing his abundant joy. "Now I'm a winner! Yahoo!"

After realizing that neighboring shop attendants were starting to poke their heads around the corner to see what all the noise was about, Jin brought Mr. Legg into the store. Almost weeping in happiness, Mr. Legg went on to confess, "I've needed to do some exercise for a long time now." Blink-blink. "My doctor says I need to do some sport, and now I won this contest, and I can try some sport for free! It's the greatest thing that ever happened to me!"

Jin explained that as was the case with all the "winners," the prize did not include sports shoes, as required by the gym where he would be training, and that validation was in conjunction with the purchase of the new Nike cross trainers, available at a reduced rate of 20 percent when Mr. Legg made the decision to buy the shoes.

Upon reflecting on the experiences of the day, Jin thought to himself, *Just when you think haven't they heard all this before, someone will come along and prove you wrong.*

That evening, Art laughed at Jin's charade of Mr. Legg's grand entrance. Jin used both hands to represent eyelids as he imitated the blink-blink effect, and the result was hilarious. Even Uncle D was nearly in tears upon hearing the tale. Seeing Jin's gestures of the client's happiness as he dropped to his knees before looking up to his uncle and saying, "It's the greatest thing that ever happened to me," put all of them in hysterics.

Jin hit a new weekly record personal best. By sculpting his conversations to cater to the traits he encountered, he was able to waste less time on time-wasters and get to the point of selling more efficiently than ever before. It had never occurred to him how simple it was to identify various dominant personality traits.

Steffi told him the next Friday, "Steven's back on Monday." It was obvious Steffi wanted to continue, but it just wasn't in the cards. A long break in their conversation took place due to the day's unfolding events. It was a busy day; nothing could be done about it.

Steffi made a point of getting back to him before he left, and she picked up where she'd left off earlier in the day. "When you meet Steven, please don't transfer out of here. Who else can I break out of Alsportraz with? Please, at least promise me that if you do go, you'll take me with you. I can't take any more of being talked down to. My sales are decent enough. What's the problem?" Then pushing her bra up, she asked, "Can't anyone look past these things? Can't they see that I'm working bloody hard and getting the best possible results in this place? I just wish I could come to work and enjoy coming here. It's horrible having …"

"Look, I'm sure they're lovely," Jin interrupted. "Anyone who can't look past your body must be very unhappy about him or herself. I don't think Mr. Czeronowsky is very happy here, either. Wishing for change isn't going to make it happen. You and I may be doing well, but that doesn't mean the store is. For the store to do well, something else needs to change. I don't know what, but it's obviously something that Mr. Czeronowsky is struggling with inside himself. All we can do is change ourselves in a way that will hopefully allow him to make those changes, which will result in a more positive working environment. All I can do is participate in bettering myself, which will better the working environment in which I find myself. You can too. After the change is facilitated, we won't have to leave."

"When you have your way, I may not want to." Steffi threw her arms around Jin and hugged him.

Mr. Steven Page would be attending the meeting, if not managing the meeting himself, the following Monday morning. It was time to meet the man Steffi held as a legend …

Working a Room

One, Two, Three, Four

Enter the Dragon, a.k.a. NSC General Sales Manager Steven Page. He was the coolest guy Jin had ever met, as in All-American cool. It was the kind of coolness that only Americans could exhibit, simply by sitting back, relaxing, chilling out, and, well, being cool. Steven had it down to an art. Each morning, he would arrive at 6:45, file his fingernails down for ten minutes, roll his neck around his shoulders for five, and mold his face into a smiling position until it was natural. Steven was never to be called Steve or Stevie for risk of his mom tearing a strip off of the person; somehow she just knew when it happened. As Steven put it, "You would get this phone call at some crazy hour from a Mrs. Page informing you that her son, Mr. Steven Page, was finishing off his MBA. She spent fourteen hours bringing him into this world, gave him the name, the *full* name she meant for him to have, and she wouldn't stand for anyone shortening it. And even though this mature voice on the other end was always respectful and always polite, you kind of got the feeling that she could take you out of this world in much less time than it took for me to be born ."

Jin had no idea what an MBA was, but it sure sounded important and cool. Almost as cool as the NBA, an organization that played a sport Jin had always wanted to see. Steven had an all-time record-breaking sales day that he hung on the back wall of his office like an athletic trophy. Framed in simple wood and anti-reflective glass, the record could be read from no matter where one sat in his office.

Steve was immaculately well groomed and had all the features of an All-American. He was athletic looking even though he hadn't done any serious sports since he left the army twenty-eight months earlier. Everybody liked Steven for some reason. He never raised the red, white, and blue and remained a decent person with a fantastic sense of humor. The nicest thing about Steve was that he really gave the impression that he was listening and that he cared about whatever people said, what they were doing, and what they were inspired to do.

"Discipline!" he'd say. "The key to success lies in creating a fantastic first impression, and that requires discipline. The army taught me that. Being self-disciplined ensures that I take absolutely no chances on that first hello. I make sure that I'm immaculately groomed. It helps me feel better about myself because I know I'm presentable. I can get focused on the tasks planned in my agenda, and as unfortunate though it may be, there's some truth to the fact that people won't buy from a pauper. You have to look the part without looking like you wanna sell somethin', y'know? There's no second chance to make a great first impression. I understand Ms. Gardner has spoken to you all about this at length, so I won't go into detail. My advice to you on the subject is simply to smile and be charming."

As Steven said the words, the entire group seemed to collectively relax and grin. Steve's expression bore a sensitivity at the mention of Ms. Gardner that seemed out of place, signaling to Jin that there was more between those two than Jin would ever know.

Jin had identified Steven as a D-type with a charisma that Jin had not yet encountered. It was as though one felt compelled to follow him. And Jin wasn't the only one affected: Whenever potential clients came in whom Steven had originally spoken to, they would only speak with Steven. They would rather wait twenty to thirty minutes and then be in a rush to sign the paperwork, just to talk with him. Other existing clients would stop by to ask Steven's permission to refer him to another client, and they'd only refer someone if they knew Steven would handle it personally.

Steven's discipline was brought into his sales-training methods. He thoroughly believed that people generally wanted to be led, and he was right. People felt better about what there was to be done when there was structure in place regarding what to do and when to do it. What made the team so successful wasn't due to the systems and structure, per se, but the personalities that Steven cultivated within his team. If Steven said, "Don't worry, son; you'll do all right," one believed him, and it happened! Things were weird that way.

It seemed that around Steven, "whether you believe you can or you believe you can't, you'll be right."

Steven seemed to have it all going his way. Being senior sales executive for All Sports meant he was in charge of personnel such as Mr. Czeronowsky—he was Jin's boss's boss, in effect. Steven was one of these guys who walked into a room, and it would light up.

Though the meeting was brief, Steven's message was simple, and Jin had to admit his smile was catchy. The man could simply mingle through a crowded room and start up conversations that got everyone finding their own solutions. Steven was fearless at meeting new people, and he did it with ruthless efficiency. Steven's handshake left an impression with Jin that he sincerely meant it when he said to him, "If you have any difficulties, come up and see me, and we'll see if we can't work it out together, my man."

The next week, Jin had been having a hard time meeting people in order to hit sales targets that week. He walked over to Mr. Page's office one morning before his secretary had arrived and asked, "Excuse me, sir, but how do you do it? How do you meet so many people? I do my best to meet as many as I can, but I cannot match your figures. I could use some help and was recommended by my colleague to ask you." Steven Page's sales figures were known to be consistently 40 percent above the other team members' back when he did sales, and Jin was eager to learn.

"First of all, Jin, congratulations on being the first person to come in my office and ask me about that. It takes courage. Now, explain to me as best you can what you believe the problem to be." He put down his nail file and eased into his chair to give Jin his undivided attention.

"How, exactly, do you meet people? I notice that you seem so at ease with it, whereas the others in the team aren't. I would like to learn from you. Please tell me, what do you do different?"

Every word seemed to go directly in to Steven's thoughts. He waited patiently for Jin to finish before answering. "I learned in the army how to pick up girls." Jin's brow furrowed, and Steven elaborated. "I apply the same techniques in getting to meet people. Getting transferred around from camp to camp gave ample opportunities to practice and refine those skills. Look, whether it was a night out with the boys in the 342nd E to try and get as many foreign telephone numbers as possible, or an official gathering of big wigs to get on the right side of who's who, the principles are the same. Don't worry about not feeling comfortable going up to strangers—it's natural. I read a survey that asked what people desired least to do in life, and dying came in third! Now, I don't know about you, but that seemed kinda low to me. I mean, *third* place? Apparently public speaking was second, and meeting a stranger in a room full of strangers was number one!

"I reckon if no one else is doing it, whether or not because they're too afraid to, it makes for a group of contact people who nobody else is tapping. What's for sure is that there's most certainly a group of people that aren't being approached that suit our target market. To me, that smells like an opportunity to build a bunch of prospects with relative ease. The tricky bit is just doin' it."

"But you make it look so easy," Jin noted.

"As with anything, that comes along with practice. Once you see it working for you, it'll motivate you to keep on going."

"So, how do you work a room?"

"Well, let me explain it to you as best I can." With that, Steven calmly went to the door and closed it, saying to the receptionist, "Suzie, hold my appointments and calls, would you, please? Just tell them I'm helping a friend, and they'll understand. Thank you." After the door clicked, he turned to Jin with an element of serious helpfulness. "Ask, Jin, and ye shall receive." That charming grin made it impossible not to smile back and feel good about having asked.

"Now then, in any given room, there are only four types of groups of people, and no more. Remember that." A simple nod and a pencil with notepad came out of Steven's desk, and he handed them to Jin before he continued. "It will never matter where you look—a club, a playground, or an office party—there will be four groups. I call them ones, twos, threes, and fours. I like to keep things as simple as possible, and to me, simple means structure. You'll only ever see groups of one person (an orphan), two people, three people, and four or more people. Easy, huh?

"I understand you've learned of or at least heard of my lectures on DISC analysis from Miss Schuld. So which DISC element would you expect to be amplified in a room full of strangers? Think about it for a moment and tell me how you would feel."

Jin replied, "I always feel shy, even though generally I am not a particularly shy person. If others were feeling much the same way

I'd say they are feeling a bit insecure unless already engaged in a conversation, so S-type?"

"Exactly! People may not *be* S-types, but much the same way vacations tend to bring up the impulsiveness or 'I' in all of us, so too do rooms full of strangers tend to amplify the S-type in everyone. We seek something familiar, something secure. Very good, my man! Now, with that in mind, all we need to do is look at the body language of any given group. What they are saying as a group? In any given group, they can be either open or closed. The general rule is that a group of one are open, and groups of four or more are generally closed.

"Picture a crowd, any crowd. Think of how they are standing about. Better yet, let's head over to the sandwich bar across the road, to see it for real." As they left his office, he said to his secretary, "Suze, just out of office to the sandwich bar for an hour with my man Jin here. Need anything?"

She said no and waved good-bye. Jin and Steven went together across the way; it was about midday, and Steven did confess to being in need of sustenance and spontaneously invited Jin along.

As they grabbed jackets, Steven wanted Jin to look about and tell him whether groups were open or closed. "By open, I mean that the group is open to meet someone new. Groups of one, or orphans, are always open. You might not be the person they're looking to meet, but they're open."

The sandwich bar was set up with standing-only tables, which gave a social atmosphere because there were not places for people to recluse from conversation. It could have been any pub or inn, but it had gone "eco" about a year ago and was still hip.

"As we're here, we might as well get something to drink." A finger waved to the girl behind the counter resulted in two cappuccinos delivered. Steven said "Just two times the regular, please, sweetheart," and soon they had two freshly made sandwiches delivered to their table without having to stand in line.

Steven continued with the lesson. "So how do you introduce yourself? Well, there are about fifteen points to keep in mind. It's not important to remember them all, because a lot of them don't really matter." Steven surveyed the room briefly. "For example, we have these caps, so we can easily take our drink and switch hands. Make eye contact and smile." Steven demonstrated the ease of the first couple of steps at the people waiting in line before turning back to Jin, where the on-site demonstration ended. "And as politely as possible, go over and ask permission to join them. Say something like, 'Do you mind if I join you?' As long as they're cool with it, you're in!

"It doesn't matter where you are—simply introduce yourself. Some keys are to use your first name only when introducing yourself, to avoid any possible ego conflicts. Be a *person* first. I can't stand it when people introduce themselves by their title, as if to say, 'Hi, I'm important. More important, I'm probably more important than you, because I do important things for other people more important than either of us.' Ugh! Most people I know agree with me that it's easier to be seen as a person first and acknowledged for what you do, than to been seen as a title first and build a relationship to later become acknowledged as a person.

"You know how to introduce yourself properly now, so let's say that's gone all right and they're not a bore. Open the conversation with something that you have in common. The easiest fact is that that until just a moment ago, you were both orphans. I always open with a question about where we are and the common thing we've most likely just been feeling until that point—something to the effect of, 'Man, these get-togethers can be a great place to meet people, don't you think?' Or, 'Boy, these places can be pretty intimidating, don't you agree?' These tips I'm about to give you will work in any situation. Whether you find yourself standing on a street corner or an invited guest to the coolest party in town, getting in with the right people is more a numbers game than an actual talent. The results of those encounters are what make all the difference."

Sensing Jin's concern, Steven continued. "Relax, my man. Just be yourself and use all your Gung Ho stuff to take care of the rest. People are at their personal best when they're being themselves. So, you know, if that's you, be the squirrel, the beaver, and the goose; all that will come in handy. Be yourself, and great things will happen—just like I heard great things were happenin' with the cleaning team. Well done!

"The thing to do is scavenge through the crowd for the nut: look for people you would like to possibly meet, and offer them the chance to meet you. People you needn't bother with are either wearing headphones or on the phone. Nobody likes to be bothered when they're on the phone. If it's important enough to them, they'll turn whatever it is they have in their ear off and get to it. By the same token, you might consider waiting for them to turn it off before continuing an engagement. For example, if someone was on the phone and wanted my attention, I would calmly state that I'll wait until they're done with their call and turn my shoulder to them to allow them the choice. If they press, I'll tell them I'm sure the person on the other end will appreciate my waiting.

"The official steps involve congratulating them on their choice and repeating the process, now as a slightly larger group. In other words, begin introducing yourself and move on together.

"Entering a group of two people works about the same, except that you need to be aware whether their body language is open or closed. Let me explain. Either people are facing one another, or they're not." Steven showed with his hands cupped, to clarify the point as he swiveled them from the heel of the palm. "Closed or open. Groups of two can choose to be one or the other. They're either open to interjection, or they're not. Just as an orphan, or a group of one, can be tuned in to a phone conversation, so too can a group of two people be turned in to a conversation with each other. How engrossed they are in each other will determine how appropriate it may be to interject, as opposed to interrupt.

"Lulls in conversation are warm zones where it's possible to get a word in, edgewise. The basic rules of social engagement are to engage first visually, then verbally, then physically—always in that order. If they haven't approached you, the rules for groups of either two or three people are essentially the same: the best you can do is maintain a charming disposition at all times. At least you'll know they'll want to get to know you.

"Groups of four or more tend to square off and are best left alone, on the whole. Not to worry, though, because they tend to break apart and re-form just as quickly.

"If you want to have a more private talk with someone, simply turn to them, and you'll naturally show the rest of the room that the conversation you're having is private. Now, if it should turn out that they're a bore, what do you do? There's this great way to get out of it, and it's the simplest of things once you know how to do it. It's considered bad manners to be the last person to talk and then leave, so all you have to do is stop talking and take a small step back from the individual or group, and listen for a while. Excuse yourself politely, either to the bar or the bathroom, depending on how eager you are to lose them.

"Simple, huh? You got all that, my man? You look as though you regret not having taken notes. We'd best be heading back, as break time is done, my man."

With that they returned, and Steven encouraged Jin to sit in Steven's office to contemplate all that had been said at lunch. "I do apologize if I've gone into too much detail for you, Jin. Working a room just happens to be a passion of mine right now, as I'm writing my thesis on it for my MBA. No one's ever been able to explain how to do that before, and I reckon this is going to be my ticket out of here. Anything else I can help you with, my man?"

Jin replied, "Yes, please. Could you explain to me what's the use of an MBA?"

Steven sighed through a smile, got up, went over to the door, and leaned to his right as he spoke in the direction of the reception desk. "I'm back now, Suzie. Any messages, darlin'? I'll have them now if I could, please."

Apparently an MBA was a master's degree in business administration that involved a huge investment in time and money. It was very challenging and took a lot of time; if one screwed it up and failed any of the courses, one had to spend more time achieving the end result. It seemed that Steven had little time to do anything other than work at his job and his degree. He was committed to doing well at both.

Oh well, thought Jin. An MBA seemed an expensive and exhaustive degree to get, and it wasn't worth anything if one didn't know how to use it, how to sell it. Still, it seemed the coolest thing to have, because Steven was going to have his within the next few months.

Jin heeded Steven's advice. He used the newly learned techniques to identify who to meet, and how to talk to people he didn't yet know. The numbers game played its hand, and at the end of the month Jin had talked to more people, and more effectively, than ever before. The result was that Jin broke his personal sales record that month, and to show his appreciation, he took Steven to a basketball game. It was Jin's first attendance at a real game, and both Jin and Steven cheered on Seattle as they whipped Vancouver. *I must never forget to thank the people who get me where I am, as best I can. Saying a thank-you doesn't mean that it has to be something remotely unpleasant that I won't enjoy as well.* Steven genuinely appreciated the gesture, in addition to getting away from writing his thesis.

Qualification

The Three Ps

"If you don't qualify them, you'll end up buying them."

Jin sat in this week's course in sales and admittedly felt a little lost as to how to respond to the opening statement. What on earth is this guy talking about?

"It's something to think about," the speaker, Mr. Czeronowsky, went on. "As you're negotiating, a sale will be made regardless. Either you will sell the person on why they'll reach a purchasing decision, or they will sell you on why they won't."

Mr. Czeronowsky spoke in short sentences paced in between breaths. Now in his early thirties, some recently gained weight was evident by the scratch marks on his belt from somewhat slimmer times. Though his breathing was rather pronounced, he was by no means an unhealthy man, nor was he particularly tall; the combination simply made things look more converse.

"In order to save a ton of time"—and Jin wondered if every reference was going to be in terms of pounds or kilos—"we can streamline the process by asking three specific questions. It's what I call, the Three-Pee-Oh formula. It used to involve two questions, but we couldn't go on calling it the Pee-Pee rule, now, could we?"

Chuckles were stifled around the room. Matt Czeronowsky just wasn't that funny a guy. Although his humor carried particular but genuine warmth, Jin found it challenging to warm up to him, and he had no idea why. He appeared normal enough with a neatly pressed shirt tucked into slacks, and dress shoes with a matching belt color. No tie and an open collar made him appear approachable enough ... but Jin was never sure that he actually would approach him. Perhaps it was just Matt's use of toilet humor. It was as though there was something sinister behind the rounded face and short blond hair.

"You can't expect to get on with everyone," Jin could imagine Uncle D saying. "So you'll have to make best with the ones around you."

Nothing to do but get on with it, Jin thought, and he imposed attentiveness on himself so as to ease the suffering.

"Past, present, and possibility," Mr. Czeronowsky wrote clearly and for all to see on a flip chart at the front of the room. His handwriting was tidy. Jin found something to like about him finally; he could focus on that.

"What's the difference between a pedestrian and a prospect? It's the little picture of the pedestrian on a lamp post that gets people to cross the road. A prospect that passes us by is no more than a pedestrian. Anyone know why the chicken crossed the road? No? Because nobody stopped it to ask ... or possibly, because no one asked it to stop."

He's getting better, Jin thought.

"My point is, we don't want to let prospects pass us by. In order to turn a pedestrian into a prospect, it helps to learn where they've been or what they've experienced in the past, so that we can understand where they're at in the present moment, so that we can establish a possible outcome, a sale. Once a possible outcome is established, that pedestrian becomes a prospect. Got it?

"The rest of the population—the pedestrians—are chickens! Let them go on squawking about their way. Stay focused with the person you are dealing with; give him or her your undivided attention as much as possible."

A hand went up across the table. "Be present, sir?"

"Very good. Yes, be there for them. Stay connected with them without getting in their face, if you know what I mean. Keeping this process as simple as possible, we can ask three open-ended questions that will get us right to the point. First, we ask where they've been. Why do you think we do that? Anyone?"

Several answers rang out around the room.

"To establish a history?"

"To break the ice?"

"To stop them from crossing the road?"

The humor had improved enough that smiles broke out across the room. Even Mr. Czeronowsky grinned as he continued. "Yes. On all accounts, yes. We want to build rapport with customers somehow. It shows interest in their dilemma. Gets them through that feeling of being the only one out there looking for whatever it is they're looking for, and it does indeed get them to at least pause from passing us by. Even more than that, it helps us know what language to use.

"During the second P phase, the present phase, we establish where customers are at so as not to bore or overwhelm them. Remember that at this point they are still pedestrians and not prospects, because potential has yet to be established. No matter what we sell, if we either overcomplicate or oversimplify, we are unlikely to close the sale. At our department in sports, for example, a woman may simply wish to firm up her hips, abs, and thighs. She's not particularly bothered to know which machine will maximize the extension and flexion of her hip adductor while supinating her abductor muscles. We may as well be speaking in a foreign language, and by adding confusion to an already perhaps difficult decision, the woman is most likely to need some time to 'think about it.' A personal trainer, however, may be looking for an edge that a supinated girdle position could give him when training his clients." Mr. Czeronowsky waved to both a man and woman at the other side of the table to give further examples. "You guys over in auto repair don't bother clients with details about the part numbers of which filters will work; the client just wants the car to stop stalling out. An enthusiast may want a somewhat higher performance part, as well as a copy of the latest Mopar catalogue.

"Once we've established exactly where the customers are, we need to know where they'd like to get to, what they'd like to achieve, change, or have repaired. Once we know this, they are now officially a prospect! All we need to do is provide them a solution to their problem—offer them a couple of options, ask which one suits them best, and then sit back and let them decide.

"So that's it. To summarize: get to know customers' past, their present situation, and their possibility, as in what they'd like to do about it."

People around Jin scribbled down notes, though few had more than "Past, Present, Possibility" on their paper.

"Within the possibility P is another hidden P—that's our 'Oh' effect. Therein lies our secret P, the purchase! As salespeople, isn't that where we'd consistently like to be?" Numerous nods of agreement and general smiles around the table indicated that that was true. "After hearing the three Ps, simply say, 'Oh, I think I might have something for you here,' and lead them toward their purchasing decision. Keep those things in mind when you go out there, and you'll have a great week!"

The general consensus was that people left the meeting room with notes of praise and thanks to Mr. Czeronowsky. Some shook hands with a simple thanks, and others mentioned that they really got something different out of the meeting. Jin felt that although time would tell what had come his way, he was pleased to be building his repertoire of things to do to sell more effectively.

The uplifted ending of the meeting left Jin feeling motivated. He had some questions regarding whether the same questions really worked for every personality. Matt Czeronowsky said, "Unfortunately I've got no time to answer that right away, though I will be sure to bring those themes to light in upcoming meetings."

Steffi was on holiday that week, which meant Jin would be responsible for the floor. It would be impossible for Jin to get any time to speak with Mr. Czeronowsky during Steffi's absence. Jin would be responsible for the entire sales figures that week and face the challenge of doubling his personal targets. Essentially, the store was too cheap to have anyone else fill in, even part time.

The following days were trying for Jin. He could work any area and was now comfortable meeting strangers. "Practice doesn't make perfect, as much as perfect practice!" he could imagine his uncle saying, although the saying was not his. Each shift was easy enough, speaking to people, but too often Jin learned that his would-be prospects had not bought anything. It created great stress for Jin because he had been looking forward to shining at the beginning of the week. To fall from that to a feeling of doubt weighed heavily on his shoulders.

Troubled and tired, Jin brought the subject up at home. Uncle D suggested Jin invest more energy trying to meet the right kind of people—people who were there to buy something. When pressed to know how to meet those types of people more effectively, Uncle D conceded that Jin had better go to whoever he could to get the expert advice he needed.

Jin could think of no one more expert than Mr. Steven Page, and so returned to his office early the next day.

This early, Jin was asked to wait while Steven concluded a telephone call before entering the office. After a warm greeting and firm handshake, Steven said to Jin, "What is the point of telling people the prices if they aren't qualified to be your customer? As silly as it seems, many people waste hours with people who don't qualify to be their customer. Put plainly, the girl looking for directions to the post office doesn't want to take advantage of the deal on shop tools. Of course, it's important to remain polite and courteous at all times, no matter what.

"There's this friend of mine in Germany who works as regional sales manager for a top-level health club chain. For their business, he's even had to take qualification to the next level—what he calls super-qualification, or Super-Q for short. Some businesses get a lot of browsers, people who genuinely just want to have a look as they pass by. They may not even live in the area, and he's had to refine his selection process to becoming a basic question of, 'Do you live or perhaps work in the area?' That way, he at least knows if a remote possibility is there to acquire a prospect.

"Introductions are wasted, and in all my years doing and coordinating promotional work, the only thing people are not offended by is a pleasant greeting. Anything else is just setting yourself up for a 'No, thank you' when you're trying to get the word out on the street about your business. Think about it—what would you say to someone who saw you in the street and said, 'Would you like a flyer, sir?' As a natural reaction Jin's answer was, "No."

"Right. There's nothing wrong with that person's politeness, so why the no?"

"Given the choice, I—"

"Exactly!" Steven jumped in to conclude. "Given the choice, most people would say no. Now tell me, would it really have made a difference if it was a girl? Scratch that. What if it were a *pretty girl?*"

It took a moment to consider, and Jin said, "I might hesitate for a moment when she spoke to me, but once I'd realized why she was speaking to me, the answer would probably be no just the same."

"That hesitation is exactly why we still put a pretty face out there on any billboard. It isn't chauvinistic or sexist to acknowledge a pretty face will affect certain elements of marketing. 'Sex sells' has been the catch phrase for the most dependent marketing-oriented business for centuries. You work together with Miss Schuld, don't you?"

Jin replied, "She is on vacation, sir."

"Well, there you have it. What's happened, my man, is that you've gone from a team of two to a team of one. Well, that *and* you've dropped in the sex factor. So stop being so hard on yourself. It's nothing to worry about. Listen, Jin, any good manager knows that one person works at, let's say, X level of efficiency. If X represents 100 percent of one person's result, then where would you expect the result of two people to be?"

"Two times. That is, twice as much," Jin assumed.

"Most people would say that. But in actual fact, a team of two will outdo that result by 50 percent, or even as much as 100 percent. So, two people end up with a result somewhere between 250–300 percent. Get it?"

"Yes, I see."

"Working backward, a good manager can plan when a team is broken up. The performance of an individual would then be the inverse, or lay somewhere between 33–38 percent of the result of the original team of two people. Do you follow me, my man?"

A comparison on paper helped Jin understand where his targets should be, and he reset his goals to allow for Steffi being away. The truth was there weren't any more people visiting the center because Steffi was away, so how could anyone expect the results to change?

Jin understood that Matt Czeronowsky must be under a lot of pressure as well. Suddenly the world was all right again. Through renewed understanding, Jin was able to see that Mr. Czeronowsky was able to approach the challenge from an entirely new direction. By approaching Matt directly, Jin was able to ask the most appropriate question. "What's the plan to make up for the fact that Steffi is away this week?"

"We're going to have to work on your tour," was the response that would lead him to greater results.

Tour

Round and Round

Mr. Czeronowsky explained his reply. "Generally, when people come into any business, one of the things they are looking for is someone who commands a certain sense of authority and knowledge. They're not doing it consciously as much as unconsciously looking to sabotage those things to make them feel better about themselves. Apparently, it is part of the self-destructive nature of our species. Ironically, no salesperson represents this phenomenon better than the shoe salesman, and there are more of them than any other type of salesman in the world.

"Consider for a moment that for centuries there have been shoes for sale. Other than sex (the oldest known profession), there is no known older sales niche, right? So you would think their sales tactics would be the most refined, wouldn't you? But think about your last experience in a shoe store. Regardless of how cool the inside of the store was, can you recall what the salesperson said when he or she approached you?"

Jin gave the expected reply. "Can I help you?"

"And what did you answer?" Matt asked.

"No thanks, just looking."

"As is the response of pretty much everyone who gets asked that question. You'd think that after centuries of sales and hundreds of thousands and millions of occurrences of asking that question, shoe salespeople would have changed their question—but they haven't, and do you know why?"

Jin shook his head and remained silent.

"Because they aren't very good salespeople. That's all. The truth is, people are going to need shoes, and shoes have been sold for so long that it's engrained in Western civilization to have many pairs of them. Over centuries, the luxury of owning more than one pair of shoes has become a social necessity; there's no demand for great salespeople in the shoe industry anymore. If you are asking people, 'Can I help you?' you can be pretty sure of their answer. So how do we get around it?" Mr. Czeronowsky took a breath before continuing. "The answer, Jin, is within ourselves. If we just think about what we want when we enter a store, the answer becomes clearer. Everyone enjoys acknowledgment. I believe Ms. Gardner talked to you about the importance of greeting people as soon as possible. There's a technical aspect of a salesperson's tour called FAB, which stands for feature, advantage, and benefit. This has to do with the salesperson's knowledge about the product or service that is being offered. FAB means nothing more than having a commonsense understanding of what the product is: its features, what it does and how it functions; the advantages as well as how it addresses the prospect's specific needs; and the benefits to the customer.

"Say a runner comes in the store looking to get some new shoes." He led Jin over to the wall of shoes in the store as he continued. "This is a shoe. Feature: it protects the foot from wear as well as weather. Advantage: it offers arch support and freedom of ankle movement with a lightweight sole compound. Benefit: it enables you, the runner, to run longer distances with less risk of injuries.

"I would suggest you go round and round the store, studying the

FAB of each item that we offer here, until you're comfortable with it. It may seem repetitive at times, and perhaps even boring, but be glad we're talking about something like sports gear and not something as complex as Boeing engines."

In between talking to prospects, Jin spent the remainder of the day, going around the store to see how "'Feature, Advantage, Benefit" could easily be applied to anything once he understood the principle.

"Got it?" Matt asked him at the end of the day.

"I believe so," answered Jin.

"Okay, here's the test. Tell me, Jin, what should a shoe salesperson be saying as they approach people?"

"Hi, I'm Jin. What is it you're looking for today?"

"F-A-B-ulous!" Matt said with a smile. "You might add: 'If there's anything you'd like a little more information about, I'll be just over here.' But it's not necessary. It's that minute difference between asking, 'Can I help?' and 'How can I help?' that makes all the difference."

The day was done, and that evening Jin left with a new understanding and renewed confidence. The only question lingering was to learn what was to be done with Steffi still being away.

The next morning, Mr. Czeronowsky admitted that there hadn't been much of a plan for Steffi's absence, and after deliberating with Jin, they agreed that the next short-term solution was for Matt himself to get out on the floor. Jin looked forward to working with him.

Mr. Czeronowsky said to Jin, "Call me Matt. When I'm on the floor, it's Matt."

The next day, Matt and Jin worked well together—so well, in fact, that Thursday's promotion nearly made up for the lost sales during the week. So many people were there that there wasn't time to get to them all. With an apologetic call, prospects were invited to come in Friday to get a last chance at the offer.

Matt knew how to use the phone effectively, and all Jin had to do was politely congratulate customers on their decision to take advantage of the mistake at All Sports and accept either cash or credit payments.

It went well, with Matt and Jin congratulating each other on a job well done. Monday would see the return of Mr. Czeronowsky, but Jin had to admit, when the chips were down, Matt pulled through.

Jin was at home asking why Mr. Czeronowsky hadn't chosen to help earlier. His uncle explained.

"The most successful people in the world, no matter how you measure their success, have gotten there because they were willing to do what no one else would. Many people end up stuck in one place because they won't do so often enough. Perhaps this is the case with Mr. Czeronowsky. Either people have a set of principles they adhere to, or they don't. Everyone can learn a set of principles that will help them do the right thing under any circumstance."

Uncle D looked at Jin long and hard. He relaxed in his chair and analyzed the situation internally before asking Jin the next question. "What were the principles of a black belt, as Sensei Iura taught you?"

Jin replied, "That's easy: CHIPSI!"

Uncle D raised an eyebrow, "And that means what?"

Jin recited his homemade acronym in full. "Courage, humility, integrity, perseverance, self-control, and indomitable spirit. I remember them well using the first letter of each word."

"Yes, yes. Very clever, Jin. It helps to build bridges, to help you remember things like that. Now, let me explain how you can apply those principles to help you outside of the dojo. Take on the challenges that are set for you either by others or yourself. No task is too menial; each plays an integral role in getting a desired result. As long as you remain humble while you carry out tasks, you will get the desired result more often. It's not going to happen every time, though; it will be trying, and you will have to persevere. Remember that the twelve-hundredth time you are answering a question, it is very likely the first time that customer is asking it, so maintain your composure. You might even be glad people have anything to ask at all, because that is a great indicator that your market exists. Be patient, no matter what. Patience may very well be the noblest outward sign we can offer people as a sign of our own indomitable spirit. Not everybody has it."

Patience
Brown Belt

The Olympic Theory

"Jin," began Uncle D, "even being at the top is not the end of your journey. Don't allow a slump to be the end, as many others do." It was apparent that a second falling of either wisdom or knowledge was about to unfold. Jin braced himself for his uncle possibly testing his martial arts training philosophies. "Remember when I brought you down to the Pike Place Market? Do you remember the fishmongers?"

"Yes, of course, Uncle." Jin recalled the enthusiasm and energy with which the fishmongers worked. They had truly established themselves as being "world famous."

"And do you recall the Olympic theory from your brown belt test?"

I knew it—another test, thought Jin. He smiled as he slowly recited; "Only a small fraction—say, 3 percent—of sports athletes have the time, talent, coaching, and resources to compete in the Olympic Games. It is the thinking, habits, and behaviors of this small and successful group that provide the example we'd want to model for success. But the other 97 percent are the majority, so the lesson is to pay less attention to the majority and look for the behaviors and attitudes of the top 3 percent."

"Uh huh," Uncle D confirmed. "Successful people don't stop once they've made it. The people you saw working at the fish market are not the original owners; the original owners have long since moved on."

Jin's brow raised, and he wanted to know what the original owners could be throwing around nowadays.

"It has been many years since I had dealings with them, Jin. The original owners applied their business principles to what has become the most popular coffee-shop chain in the world today!"

"Throwing coffee?" The perplex on Jin's face could be read easily enough.

"You know it as Starbucks, my boy! Starbucks now has over ten thousand shops around the world, and it is still growing at a phenomenal pace. Although the only principles you might notice as a customer are in the way the coffee drinks are shouted back at one another, I assure you they are all there. Remember your teachings. It took courage to venture into an unfamiliar area all those years ago. Courage to do so with such humility so as not to boast publicly that the business is theirs. I'm not sure anymore, but I do have the understanding that at least one of the original founders, Howard Schultz, is still somehow involved, possibly still the majority shareholder.

"Years ago, one of my employees got word of a possible change of the Starbucks logo and he approached them immediately thinking of the prestige it might offer. His pitch failed miserably, and we lost them to another client. Our dealings with Starbucks helped me understand what integrity they operate with, and how it can help grow a company to epic proportions. It was with integrity that they explained that the Siren depicted on the logo was not to be changed. It was with integrity that they shared with us their romantic visions of seafarers bringing the fresh coffee to the shores and to their cafés. They weren't going to give that up. Even while other marketing companies persisted that changing the logo was the right thing to do, their board of directors showed great tolerance and self-control. That wood-cut Siren that protected the sailors was to stay, and it was decided with much passion, much indomitable spirit.

"In the end, they went with another marketing company that shared their vision more closely; the company they chose to go with was the only of the group that talked about using recyclable products. Their bid may have been higher, but the integrity that they persevered with was so great that there truly was no other option. The only noticeable changes they ended up making were to remove where it used to say 'Coffee, Tea, and Spice' to say 'Coffee,' and Starbucks went immensely eco-friendly.

"I learnt a valuable lesson then about integrity. It will be challenged, and it is only by holding on with conviction to your integrity that you will grow. It is the thinking, habits, and behaviors of people like Howard Schultz that provide an example for modeling success. Pay less attention to the majority and look to his behavior and attitude and how things surrounding him have grown. Starbucks, my boy—that's growth!"

Jin thought of his uncle's words. His speeches always inspired him somehow, so much so that he could hardly wait to get back to work.

Jin was ready to take on whatever the world threw at him Monday morning. He stopped by Steven's office to thank him for his help the other day. He was eager to share how the events eventually unfolded, and the turnaround that had been made at the store. Again he was politely asked to wait. The receptionist was certain Steven would like to hear Jin's tale and would be grateful for the note of thanks. Apparently sales management was rather thankless.

"Fantastic!" roared the comment out of Steven's office as a very loud phone conversation came to an end. Everyone within earshot was respectfully eager to know what Steven was so excited about. Equally, those within earshot were anxious to know what was going to be said, as Steven poked his head out from behind the door and called out, "Jin? Come here, my man." Steven's face was equipped with that charming smile. "I've got something for us, something big. Come on inside for a minute." Jin was already smiling, but Steven's energy had Jin too curious to remember what it was he had come in for originally. The receptionist nodded, knowing that she would be hearing soon what all the fuss was about. Jin could always tell Steven his good news later.

However, Steven wasn't budging on his news until hearing Jin out about his. "That's fantastic! Well done to both of you. And you were able to convince Matthias to get out of that office and do something about the situation? That is good news! Excellent!"

"I think I know just the thing to congratulate you with …" Steven's words trailed off as he spun around in his chair for dramatic effect. He whipped around once before snapping both hands out, pointing directly at Jin. He looked to the door, shut from prying secretaries, as he spoke. "I've just got off the horn with a buddy of mine in Germany: Michael Arneson. Ever heard of him? I think I might have mentioned him to you?" A twist of Jin's lower lip and raised eyebrow revealed he had no idea who Michael was. "No matter. Mike's become a bit of a legend over there as this master sales-management trainer, and he has this new seminar going on all about referrals and getting a referral business system in place. The thing is, people are paying four hundred bucks to get into this seminar.

"I think you're ready for it, my man. I want you to come with me. The NSC will pick up the cost of flying. It'll be great! It's about time you learned about referrals, anyway. Why not have some fun while we're at it? I may be a sales manager, but Mike's a sales master. He used to say to this other guy who would criticize him, 'You haven't made a sale until you've mastered a sale.' In Germany, he's become a sales guru. He thinks it's hilarious!"

Another plane trip across the world? Jin thought. *Hilarious ...*

Enthusiasm
Brown-Striped Belt

The Two Qualities of a Champion

- Attention to detail
- Follow-through

Jin didn't have a lot of time to explain the situation to Mr. Czeronowsky because there was much to be done at the store. Admittedly, Matt had been doing well and had abandoned much of his office work. His mood had been getting better as his esteem returned. He agreed it was good timing—Jin would leave as Steffi returned. That meant they would not be short-handed..

Mr. Czeronowsky had been toying with an idea to hire more part-time sales people on a commissions-only basis; his theory was that more sales people meant more sales. No sales for a commissioned salesperson meant no additional expenses for his department, which was favorable. Paid-on-performance, or P-on-P, was a viable way to test the market more aggressively. As Mr. Czeronowsky shared his thoughts with Jin, it seemed he wasn't sure if he meant to assure Jin or reassure himself more. "The real challenge will be controlling them. As freelancers, they are a potential threat to the good name of our department. It means I'll be on the sales floor more, which I'd like. And I'll be responsible to make sure they don't tread on either your or Steffi's toes, which will benefit you two."

The P-on-P plan was particularly interesting in that it meant earnings weren't limited in any way. It was apparent that Matt meant only for the best to happen in his department. He even spoke concernedly that Steffi and he might find a way of working together respectfully, and he welcomed the possibility.

Jin's concerns, however, were at another altitude.

"I'm a little nervous about the flight." Even as he said it, a bead of sweat ran down the base of his spine.

"I admit it's a long flight and they aren't that comfortable, but there's nothing to worry about," said Matt. "Besides, flying's one of the safest forms of travel today. Get on the Internet and find out for yourself. Then get on that plane and follow through on what you've learned."

The environment at All Sports had changed, and for the better. Jin wouldn't see Steffi before it was time to leave. That was the way of things sometimes; two ships that passed …

Getting on a plane again was a surreal experience for Jin. After carefully scrutinizing the Internet, he had learned that, statistically, planes were safer than automobiles and that there had never been an accident caused by air turbulence. It was details like that, that helped

Jin follow through. His fear of flying subsided. That same residual fear was changing into an opportunity for accomplishment.

Changes, including Jin's passion for living life, had occurred since his original flight to Seattle. The ripple effect of his conversation with Art had lessened the size of the swell before him.

"No waves," Jin commented quietly with a faint smile.

"What's that?" Steven asked as he pulled off his headphones, to be sure he hadn't missed anything.

"Nothing, just an inside joke. No big deal. I was just commenting on how calm things are going."

The airplane headphones now rested on Steven's collar. "My man, any idiot can pilot a ship through calm waters; it the heroes that take on the storm. Life's a lot like that too. Mike lives his life for the storms. You'll meet him and like him. He's the kind of guy who's at his best when he's grappling the bull by the horns. He can't stand the calm—he'll chase down a storm just to ride it out. Never a dull moment, that's for sure!

"He's unbelievable. I look up to the guy for what he's accomplished. And to think, he started with next to nothin'. Flew to Europe with a plane ticket and four hundred bucks in his hand. (That's Canadian dollars, by the way, and they ain't worth a thing anywhere else in the world.) Then, just to top that off, he goes and cashes in on his return plane ticket for a bit more—what he calls incentive to do well on the other side of the world. Couldn't speak a word of German and had no job. The guy's utterly amazing."

Jin realized that he'd never heard Steven speak so highly of someone before. It used to be that if Steven gave the slightest compliment about anyone, people would just instantly like that person without having met him or her. It was unusual to hear Steven looking up to anybody.

"Listen, Jin, we've got a rather long flight, and I guarantee a full schedule in Cologne, so get as much rest as you can. You're going to wish you had, if you don't." And with that the headphones went back on, and Steven slipped into a bit of a trance for the rest of the flight.

Curiosity kept Jin awake most of the trip. Steven awoke to about 60 percent capacity during the layover in New York—enough to get up out of one airplane seat and plunk down into a seat inside the waiting area. A shame, really, because even though the day was dreary, it was easy to feel the aliveness of the city. The buildings were huge, bigger than he ever could have imagined possible. Jin had seen pictures, of course, but being there made all the difference on the scale of it all. The immensity of the uniquely understated architecture and reinforced concrete designs, all for housing New York's hustle and bustle. It was no wonder the city never slept. Steven, on the other hand, batted an eyelid on hearing that the flight was to be delayed approximately twenty minutes.

Other than the slight delay, the continuing flight was uneventful. Five half-watched movies later, they were approaching their final destination: Cologne.

As they approached the foreign country, Jin had a chance to review his manners and be on his best behavior, as his mother would have wanted him to be. It was important that Jin be polite at all times to the best of his ability. Jin could still hear the words in his head as though they had been spoken just the other day. "If you haven't anything nice to say about anyone, it's best not to say anything. Good morals are guided by your ethical conduct. Choosing words wisely is just as important as how you say them," his mother would say. "It's not all that's necessary to become a just and moral person, but cultivation of right speech will help stay the path. The importance of speech in the context of our family's Buddhist ethics is obvious: words can break or save lives, make enemies or friends, start war or create peace. Promise me you will abstain from false speech, especially telling deliberate lies. Say you will neither slander nor use words maliciously against others. You needn't ever use harsh language that may offend or hurt others. And last but not least, abstain from idle chatter that lacks purpose or depth."

Her words had helped sculpt Jin into the person he was: a young man who told the truth and spoke in a warm, friendly, and gentle way, as well as speaking only when necessary.

"Köln," said Steven, now coming out of his sedated state upon hearing the announcement to fasten their seat belts. Not entirely convinced at the native English speaker's translation in German, Steven corrected the faux pas. "It's pronounced 'Kull'n.'"

"You speak German?" Jin asked.

"I *am* German. I was born in Munich—that's München to me. My father was in the military and married an American girl, my mom. I grew up in the States and served in the German militia. I did my tour and was disheartened by my experiences, so I left, honorably. Anyway, I met Michael after getting out of a job rut over here. Couldn't help but like the guy, though we had our conflicts, of course."

An announcement came throughout the cabin, and the anticipation was stifling.

Steven said, "Willkommen in Köln, Kumpel. Welcome to Cologne, my man. Here, you try sayin' it. Say 'Kull'n.'"

"Cul'n."

"Not bad. Now try saying, 'Kull'sh.'"

"Kölsch."

"Perfect!" Jin could feel Steven's tempo picking up to his usual speed. "Jin, my man, with that, you're ready for Germany!"

It was good to get some fresh air after the flight. Though the airport was enclosed, it was obvious that the weather was fantastic. The cleanliness of the airport struck Jin. Cologne International Airport boasted lots of glass and steel. Here they were, across the globe at the doorstep of Germany's largest city, the million-people city, as it was apparently known. Evening was blowing across the skies, and in an hour it would be dark.

Michael Arneson greeted them at the airport, to ensure they found their way. He immediately brought them out of the way of the other arriving passengers, and over to the neighboring café for a welcomed stretch and break.

Steven had surveyed the café and had already invited a couple of female travelers over for espressos. Jin greeted Michael. "Hi, I'm Jin. I'm very pleased to meet you. From all the good things Steven's been saying about you, I expected you to be at least six foot two!" Jin had no troubles adopting the lightheartedness and addictive smiles of both gentlemen.

"You'll have to forgive my attire—I'm dressed a bit casual today. Perhaps if I'd worn my tie, you'd think bigger of me?" A tie was the only piece missing from his ensemble. A smartly cut beige suit with an open collar gave a sharp and upbeat look that couldn't be denied. Michael stood about five foot ten. Jin's first meeting with a Canadian here in a German airport, though unusual, set for Jin a mental standard of what Canadians should look like. Michael had medium-length dark blond hair that waved about his face. Ruddy, near golden skin and an immaculately clean-shaven face gave Michael an appearance of the alpha wolf without an ego. Michael's jaw was accented by the permanent semismile that grew as he listened to conversation. Michael's eyes would pierce for the truth and understanding as evidenced by all the attention they gave as one spoke to him. A girl he briefly spoke to had already commented, "You have lovely green eyes. How compassionate you must be!"

And that was in response to a simple, "Excuse me, miss, would it be all right if my colleagues and I sat here? They've had a long flight, and I'd sure like to catch up with them a bit while they take a load off."

"We all can't be as big as Steven here," Michael said with that entrenched smile, the kind with the lines on the face that someone only earned after years of it being there. He admirably patted Steven on his stomach. After numerous hugs and slaps on the back, with things said in German to each other in obvious astounding and mutual admiration, it was obvious that Michael was genuinely happy to see them. "You see, friend, I'm sure you're just as big as me."

"Round here, we're not measured in feet and inches." Mike made a dramatic pause, ensuring that a couple of smiles came from the new additions to their group. "Round here, people are measured by the size of their heart. Isn't that right, girls?" More giggling assured them that indeed it was the case.

Raising his glass, Steven spoke first. "Cheers, pal. Gosh, it's good to be back. Great to see you!" Another flurry of hugs took place. Somehow, the two girls got swept into the fold. "Wait till ya see where I've got you two checked into. You're staying at the Plaza—it's lush! You two ladies all right for a place to stay this evening? Good. If you've nothing planned, we're going out for sushi at Media Park. It's the best little place on the corner, with live-action sushi chefs in the middle of an island serving you. I'd be insulted if you two aren't my honored guests. Here's my card; call me in thirty minutes with an answer, and we'll go. It'll be fun."

It went that naturally for Michael. He told the two men, "Let's get you checked in, and then we'll celebrate your arrival." A cell call later, they were on their way to the hotel in a cab.

The Plaza Hotel in Cologne had recently been renovated and was making its best effort to become Germany's first six-star hotel. They were warmly received, and Michael assured them that he would be back in thirty minutes to show them the sites.

"It'll be a long evening," Steven cautioned Jin. "There's a good chance it'll be the first of the all-nighters. Michael doesn't stop, ever! I don't know what fuels him, but I've never seen him tired."

They went to Sukashi's Sushi House, where they found the girls waiting. The view from the outside corner helped Jin understand why Media Park was such a feature of Cologne's architecture. The giant steel buildings were immaculately laid out, each rising up from the common central area and fanning back with enormous walkways between the buildings. It was well suited for traffic, although none was to be found. The park was strictly a pedestrian-only zone.

"From a helicopter, it would all look like a big piece of cheese. What you'd realize is that some of the pieces are missing. The design sends a pretty clear statement into the corporate world. It reminds me of the architect's joke about having his piece of the pie."

Steven said, "You all can have yours, but I'm taking my share first!"

"Exactly!" Michael confirmed Steven's understanding of the understated. The two of them laughed as they got into old times. The girls were pleased enough to be looked after and treated with respect.

Michael claimed to be no connoisseur but knew what he liked. "I recommend we try the Riesling; it goes well with the food here. The Germans know more about wines than you and I. It's just come into season and ought to be just right."

An agreed wine order from Rheinhausen arrived. The wine from the Rhine region was refreshing and clean, a great complement to the food. Talks went on about the taxations of wines and why the French came out ahead at the end of it all, and the Germans were stuffed. Dinner went on for hours in Germany, and it was by no means time unpleasantly spent. In fact it was made more than enjoyable by the sincerity of the company one shared.

Enjoyment and pleasure had so much importance placed on it by the German people, and the sushi house was well suited for their rendezvous this evening. The chefs were an animated lot, speaking as quickly in German as they did in Japanese, much to Jin's amusement. Though their English was not as strong, the food took no extra time to prepare. Dishes constantly traveled around a central island that housed the chefs, to entice customers. People simply took what they wanted and left the rest.

"Not a bad philosophy for living life, if you ask me," said Steven. "Take what you want and leave the rest. Life is too short to do it all."

The group nodded in agreement. Michael's smile broadened, and he slung his arms in a friendly manner around the girls as he continued the thought. "I'm doing just that." The release of his tug on the girls' waists let everyone in on the humor of the jest, and they all broke into laughter.

"Okay, it's getting late." Steven seemed shocked to hear Michael say that. "They mean to close for the evening. So, next we're going on to a Persian bar. Are you girls game to go to a club?"

A quick word with each other resulted in nods, and the group called another taxi. It arrived a short while later, and as they were piling into the available spaces, Jin queried the others quite innocently about how it was possible that Europeans called cabs taxis, which kept them merry for the rest of the journey. Jin would be able to vouch for the merriment of the colleagues during the rest of his journey.

He had decided to return to the hotel for his first night in Germany. They agreed that Steven would brief him on whatever he missed if there was anything … significant. Regardless, one taxi stop later, Jin was on his way to get some rest in an amazingly comfortable bed.

Steven wouldn't return until the wee hours of the morning. They were soon to be ready and didn't have much time to prepare. They had the day to enjoy the city sights, including the infamous Dom Cathedral. Michael wanted to spend the day with them and had agreed to meet shortly after breakfast. "Get a workout in, and you'll be fine," Steven said. "Ship shape and shaven in two hours, and he'll meet us both afterward in the lobby. What did he say? Oh yeah. We're to let Jenna know who we are when we're done."

The health club therein was gorgeous. It was arguably the hotel's sixth star because it ran independently from the hotel, although they operated from the same building. For all its luxury, it was easy to feel at home in this place. An ozone-filtered pool boasted no chlorine, polished granite countertops were framed by the smiles behind the reception desk, and a girl wearing a name tag marked Jenna offered an amazing number of towels to each of them for their use at the full-service facility.

"Why so many towels?" Jin inquired.

A smile on Steven's face let Jin know something was up, just as his answer confirmed. "Trust me, my man. Just relax and go along with it." He indicated the smaller towel as they were changing, "Bring only this one out to train with, and you'll enjoy yourself. It'll do you good."

It was true. The workout really did do the mind and the body good.

For cleanliness, the smaller towel was used to clean off the various benches used. Perspiration could be cleaned up with a sanitizing spray and paper towels found at stations throughout the gym. It was still early enough that the facility seemed relatively empty.

Steven jumped on a treadmill to go for a run. He ran and ran, and ran some more. Jin warmed up with some rowing on a rowing machine, a new experience for him, and he did some calisthenic exercises in one of the studios before meeting Steven afterward for a swim in a pool that didn't smell like a pool.

"It's ozone-filtered water—there is no chlorine, my man," Steven explained. "There are different health regulations in different countries, and Cologne has gone as eco-friendly as it can."

"Köln," Jin practiced.

"Indeed," Steven said with a smile. "C'mon, let's get you a lesson in what it means to be European." With that, Steven brought Jin around to the thalasso-area behind the pool. "This is a European sauna facility. People go into it naked—mixed, you understand? Men and women, together. It's actually not considered hygienic to wear clothing in a sauna because bacteria can incubate. That's why we received so many towels, my man. Everyone either sits or lays on one while in the sauna or on the relaxation chairs, while saving one other towel to dry off with once they're done. You can hang your shorts over there." He indicated an area over by some open showers. "Just remember to stay cool when women start taking off their towels. The naked body isn't taboo here. By shedding clothing, we shed aggressive behavior, perhaps even aggressive thoughts. I'll walk you through how to really enjoy a sauna. You with me?"

Nudity by some was seen as something perverse. Martial arts generally taught that the body was a vessel through which movement was a means of expression. The wholesomeness or unwholesomeness of actions were a matter of context. In times of training, ancient warriors would perform bodily movements that were (and still are) seen as artistic and sometimes even beautiful. In contrast, in times of war, the warriors of old performed acts of horrific violence and terrible gruesomeness. It was all a matter of perspective.

Admittedly, entering an environment while nude, with everyone else in that same environment also nude, could be unnerving. But luckily for Jin, that environment was set up to create a wholesome atmosphere where it was more natural to have a sound mind.

The ideal sauna complex expressed an environment that abstained from sexual misconduct. Point-source lighting and soft music stripped away thoughts of stealing, robbery, fraud, deceitfulness, and dishonesty. One wished no harm to come to sentient beings and would not harm others.

There were saunas of varying temperatures to be used incrementally, steam baths to be used for clearing the lungs, and cold baths to strengthen the immunity system, as well as cool-water flows and buckets filled with ice-cold water to awaken the senses. There was no room for unwholesome actions to take place. Everywhere there was space to act kindly and compassionately, to be honest, to respect the belongings of others, and to keep relationships harmless to others.

Jin was grateful to have a guide to show him how to take the right actions at the facility. By alternating between warm and cool, hot and cold, dry and wet, and then relaxing for an equal amount of time in between cycles, or courses, the body found its equilibrium. By increasing the temperature differences, one conditioned the body. For hygienic purposes, they showered in between courses.

"By encouraging the body to go to these extremes, we find balance in ourselves," said Steven as they laid back after three courses in and out of the various saunas, the last course being finished by a splash resulting from a pull on a rope attached to a wooden bucket filled with the coldest of waters Jin had ever known. Deep relaxation seeped through every pore of Jin's being as he sank away into the deckchair beneath him.

Jin's conservatism was evident in that he preferred to keep his towel wrapped about him, though he had no particular reason to be inhibited. In between courses, this appeared to be the norm; it was only in the respective rooms that one was nude with others. And not just others, but strangers. *Strange, that.*

Stranger still was the voice calling out to him, as Jin stood with his head beneath one of the showers in an open area for his final wash, before getting ready for the day ahead. Jin's body was in a deep, warm, and relaxed state. The water neatly muffled the female voice behind him saying something most likely meaning "Excuse me," as a slender young woman reached past him to the shower gel dispenser by his shower. She pressed twice for some gel and then took up a place under the shower head next to him, to wash out her hair. Everything was very aux naturelle.

Jin had always thought of German women as being somehow masculine, hearing that they were somewhat butch, or at least big-boned. *Aren't they all blonde or something?* Everyone he knew thought German girls had unshaven armpits. Yet here before him stood this petite-framed, raven-haired beauty. As she carefully washed her hair, it was revealed to Jin that German girls did indeed shave their armpits. He couldn't help but notice that German girls were perhaps even more completely shaven than Western girls. This dark-haired beauty smiled sweetly, looked Jin up and down, and then closed her eyes as soap suds started to fall over her face, offering Jin a chance to glance. It was a shame that he had to be on his way! Jin's image of German girls had changed in that instant. This was an experience to share at the dinner table back home. Art would be envious of Jin's situation.

Jin headed back to the hotel room for his calisthenic training, where he could ask himself about the righteousness of his livelihood. Jin's livelihood was indeed such that he was earning his living in a righteous way, and any wealth earned was legally and peacefully gained. In no way was he harming others by his actions. It wasn't as if he was dealing in weapons or selling people for slave trade or prostitution. So what if he was surrounded by people in the nude? He was equally exposed. Jin's mother never wanted him to work as a butcher or in any factory raising animals for the purpose of producing meat. He was never inclined to do that, so there was never really the risk of dishonoring her. Furthermore, she never meant for Jin to have any livelihood that would violate the principles of right speech and righteous action. Politics was out. The selling of intoxicants and poisons, such as alcohol and drugs, were such clear illnesses in morality and judgment for Jin that his mother had always hoped that his actions would show others the error of their ways.

Jin's livelihood was simple and pure. He felt as pure as the breath rushing in and out of him as the ritual training continued. "There is no drug that can create as great a high as the one you can create for yourself naturally." Jin felt his mother's words flowing through him, and he completed the last of the day's 150 press-ups. The way he was feeling about the day's developments, Jin would never doubt the wisdom of her words. It was a great topic for conversation, should the opportunity present itself.

Today would be Michael's turn to open up the conversation at the table. "Truth be known, you never know who will and who won't buy with absolute certainty. You can never judge a book by its cover."

"Very true!" interjected Jin, with an added recollection. "I was helping a lady who had come to me inquiring about where the restrooms were. I would've said she was of First Nations descent. She wore no visible signs of wealth and appeared to me to be more of an 'alternative' type of person. I'm sure you've all seen the type: slightly older, robust, and with a kind of a muumuu dress or something. Oh, and I remember lots of jewelry bits jangling."

Nods from around the room prompted Jin to continue the tale.

"Well, I wasn't otherwise occupied with anything pressing, so I decided to exercise my training skills. I told her it was a little complicated to describe the way, but I'd be more than happy to escort her there, if she'd allow me. The lady was gracious in accepting. She asked my name as we went along and was pleased that a youthful boy would take the time to help her. She asked who my manager was and wanted to put in a good word for me for my efforts, to which I assured her there was no need. She then asked what I did there, saying there should be more managers like me around. She then mentioned to me that she was an artist—a painter, in fact.

"I asked her if she'd seen our art supplies. She said she had not but would be glad to do so after a quick trip to the lavatory. I patiently waited before bringing her over to our art department. She had no idea we stocked her favorite product line of oils, and she had been considering trying another brand with some reservation. I had thought the line of oils a bit expensive—at least they were for me at the time—and I suggested to the woman she could put the lot on layaway. I did not make an assumption directly, but I considerately offered that our layaway plans could suit any budget if a direct purchase wasn't possible at the time. She looked at me considering what to do, and then she took the whole lot! She picked out two series of oil paints complete with the hardwood cases. She had to have every color in both sizes of tubes, just in case we ever discontinued our stock." Jin winked to let Steven and Michael know where the suggestion came from. "She chose three new easels and about a dozen or so canvases of various sizes, feeling newly inspired by her find and my help. It was a bill of a couple of thousand dollars. Then from nowhere, she flipped out a gold card and asked if it could all be delivered to her home. I explained it was no problem at all and that a small delivery surcharge would ensure that her products arrived intact. I managed to throw in a cedar blotting board for free, and she was over the moon.

"It was only after she'd left that the cashier asked me how I knew her. Obviously, I didn't.

"'That was Madame Amos Kennedy,' she explained. 'She's one of the artists exhibiting at the city art gallery right now. She's quite well-known and very successful!'

"'Oh,' I said. 'To me, she was a potential customer.'"

Steven said, "That's sales, Jin, what you've just described there!. That is sales, my man." He was nodding to Michael for a second opinion.

"You betcha! Sales is all about always, and I mean always, focusing on the task at hand no matter what. If you pay attention to the basics and stay true to them as you follow through, you will inevitably create the most successful outcome."

Ah yes, the basics. Jin was reminded of a a time in training when his patience for reviewing the basics was tested. Sensei Iura used to go over basic movements repetitively. Apparently there were only two different kicks, for example: the push kick and the snap kick. All other kicks were variations or combinations of these two kicks. Simply by changing the direction of the kick, a front kick became a side kick or a back kick. By changing direction during the kick, a snap kick became a crescent or a roundhouse kick. And by emphasizing different elements of a snap kick, the hook kick was discovered. Foot and body position determined the rest—both the starting and ending foot positions, for example, changed whether a kick traveled 180 or 360 degrees … And of course, jumping could be added for show.

The showmanship in sales for the modern-day warrior was in

attentively applying basic techniques to the unique situations that one faced every day. It was a frustrating process. Reviewing the basics of any skill could become tedious and seem boring to anyone, if not for the understanding words, "Patience, pal. We all have room to improve. It'll come." The words could have just as well been spoken by Sensei Iura.

Jason Griffiths

Determination and Follow-Through
Blue Belt

Question: What is the largest room in the world?

Answer: The room for improvement.

Being on the other side of the world meant that Jin might actually be closer to Osaka than Seattle. Whether maps would confirm or defer his feelings of closeness, Jin dreamt not of his home in Seattle, but of his home from what seemed like ages ago.

In his dream, Jin was perhaps seven years old. As a small boy, Jin used to hate cleaning his room. The excuse he used to tell his mom at the time was, "But, Mom, my room is too big!"

Jin's mother told him that if he could tell her the name of the biggest room in the world, he wouldn't have to clean his own that day—and that if he could clean that room perfectly, just once, he wouldn't have to clean his room ever again.

Sensei Iura had the answer for him as Jin tested for his blue belt. When asked what the biggest room in the world was, students were required to answer, "The room for improvement."

Jin was fighting with himself to give the answer that he knew but couldn't speak. His mouth wasn't working, and the more Jin struggled, the harder it got to speak. He would have to give the answer before time ran out, before he missed the opening of the seminar.

Seminar?

Sitting up abruptly, Jin found himself at Michael's seminar at the Plaza in Cologne, Germany, alongside a couple of hundred other people. Interesting enough, Jin's dream was the core of Michael's opening of his seminar that very day.

"No matter how good we think we are, there is always some element of our lives that we can improve upon to make us better individuals."

The seminar room Jin found himself in was spacious. It had an old theater kind of appeal with a raised stage. An area directly in front of the stage may have at one time housed an orchestra. New architecture and neutral tones of gray were accented by the blue cushioned seats, which were comfortable enough for Steven to doze in as Jin listened intently.

Michael was in his element; it was evident from the beginning. Michael's gist and step had swagger, and he stood taller somehow, more alive as though the lights that shone down on him fed him their energy. "I am here today, to instruct each of you how you can better yourselves, better your abilities as salespeople, and better the experience of your prospects with you."

There was an eight-hour time difference between England and Japan. Steven and Jin had been en route for about eighteen hours, and jet lag had finally hit Jin hard. The eastward journey did mean Jin's sleeplessness presented an opportunity to call home in the middle of the night.

"Gran," he said, "I miss mother."

"She is very proud of you."

The simplicity of Gran's words never ceased to amaze him. She had a way of putting everything in such clear perspective. "Whenever you miss her, dear Jin, you need only look in the palm of your hand, and you will see her there. Your body is her gift to you. It is part of her, even part of me, and so we all live on forever." Although tired from their conversation, Jin was pleased to know that his mother was watching over him and could always be there for him.

Jin's thoughts spun round and round …

Handling Objections

Know the Five Nos

Back at the seminar, Jin was able to focus on the rest of what was being said. Glancing at his hand gave Jin an inner peace and revitalized his attention span.

Michael said, "As most of you here already know, there are only five reasons why people say no to buying our product. The old adage of 'A person only says no five times' may be based on this simple truth." A giant screen and overhead projector allowed Michael to make notes for all to see. "Some of you may choose to make notes; others may not. I would invite each of you to take what you want and leave what you don't from your experience today."

He wrote "Five Nos" at the top of the screen.

"Anybody know them?" Various calls from throughout the auditorium filtered to the front of the room. "Too expensive? Okay, how about we write money?" He wrote it as point number five.

"What's that? Time? How do you mean?" Jin could not hear the response from where he was sitting. Some discussion brewed until Michael continued, "Ladies and gentlemen, it would seem we have two different forms of time: one involving 'not having enough time,' and the other being a fear of committing to an extended period of time. We'll call these four, time, and three, commitment." They were noted on the screen for all to read.

Michael pointed into the crowd and inquired, "What was that you said a moment ago, sir? 'I have to check with my wife or husband'? Shall we say spouse?" Point number two appeared.

"And the number one reason for people to not make a decision to buy or purchase our product or service is …?"

Many voices chorused something out, which was loosely translated on the screen as, "Need to think about it." People around the room nodded together with some mumbling, and they agreed to challenge Michael for a solution for the last point.

"Now then," Michel continued, "that's it. There are no other reasons for people to say no. It's either money, time, commitment, spouse, or they need to think about it. Agreed?"

Jin could think of no other reasons that didn't fall into the five broad categories. The question was, where was Michael going with all of this?

"Now, my good people, what if there was a way to erase all of those reasons? Are we agreed that we undoubtedly would sell more? It stands to reason that if there is no reason to say no, the only logical alternative is a yes." Pretending to hold a pipe, Michael threw in a thick English accent to change the pace as he rhetorically queried, "That's all very well, Mr. Holmes, but how do we erase these objections?" Changing his position on the stage, Michael turned sideways to face where he had just stood to answer himself. "Why, it's elementary, my dear Watson. You all have your fields of expertise, and perhaps a different product or service, but we all have one thing in common: we all sell. We are all salespeople, each and every one of us.

"The receptionist who sells an appointment at a certain time on a certain date to a patient. The guy behind the counter who asks, 'Ya want fries with that?' The video store where you live that's running membership options to save you money. The auto mechanic. The builder. Even a piece of marketing that is supposed to sell that someone calls, or comes by, or subconsciously thinks of your product every time someone asks what soft drink you'd like to drink. And yes, even the car salesperson has, on occasion, been known to sell something."

Chuckles and laughter abounded at the imagery Michael created.

"Mr. Watson's question is a valid one, and Mr. Holmes's answer is equally justified. Five questions for five objections. That's a fair trade, I'd say. Five questions, ladies and gentlemen. Therein are our answers. The answer is that we do what all great salespeople do: we ask the right questions." Putting on his best Darth Vader voice, Michael emphasized the point "Our power lies within the question. It is the true power of our sales force! Join me. Come to the smart side."

With an outward stretched arm, Michael had the crowd right where he wanted them. "Bollocks, I say! If we can't do our job better, then we must be dead! There is always a way. Ladies and gentlemen, this is the way. At the front end of our sale, we can add immense value to our sales process. I'm talking about preclosing. I'm talking about black-hole-density weight for value tipping the scale in our favor. For each of the objections, there is a question we can ask that will avoid our getting locked into the NLP close. I'll be reviewing NLP and improving on that system in part two of this seminar."

Jin had no idea what NLP was, but he was comforted that it would be explained to him in tomorrow's seminar.

"We've listed as our number five, money. In the case of smaller financial commitments, it may not be appropriate to ask, 'Do ya got any money?' We have to be discreet about it." He took a sip of water, which left a space for comment from the front rows of the room. Nodding to someone in the front, Michael smiled to respond, "Not that kind of discreet, miss." Jin thought the woman looked suspiciously similar to one of the ladies from the sushi house. "In the case of a sales representative, or an otherwise representative of a larger company making a purchasing decision, budgets can and should be discussed openly, or at least, as openly as possible.

"So what can we ask the little guy? NLP may work in most circumstances, but how about asking if customers planned to use it before, after, and during work? At least then you'll know if they have a job, and thereby an income. That ought to eliminate the objection of money being a particular issue later. Chances are if they've been thinking about it for some time, they are likely to have been saving for it for about 20 percent of that time. We'll come back to that point later.

"Time, ladies and gentlemen. Many people feel or even claim not to have enough of it." Michael paused for dramatic effect as he panned around the room. "Yet mysteriously, others do have enough. How is that possible? You, sir. Yes, you in the hat there; the gentleman with a beard. Thank you. How many hours are there in your day, sir?"

The obvious answer was shouted back: "Twenty-four."

While continuing his pan around the room, Michael selected a few other members of the crowd to answer the same question. He feigned puzzlement at the answers, which all came back the same, until he ended his tour with one woman. "You there, the lady in the white blouse and red scarf. How many hours in your day?"

In a thick German accent, the woman responded, "Zwenti-four."

With hand on his chin in a deep pondering stance, Michael asked anyone in the crowd to put up their hand who had either more of less than twenty-four hours in his or her day. When no one responded, Michael continued. "Then *surely* some of you must have either more or less than seven days in your week. Anyone? No? How bizarre!" Michael let the point sink in further before paraphrasing himself. "You mean to say that all of you have the same number of hours in your day? The same minutes in your hours, and days in your week? That's *so* weird! I know I must work something like an eight-day week. Anyone else feel that way?"

Most of the hands in the room shot up.

"Ah ha! I see. So what we're talking about is *perceived* time. Just as all of us can feel that our time is in short supply, the truth is we use our time doing the things we value the most for that moment. We must be sure our prospects place the necessary value on our product or service, or at least enough to invest in it. And how do we do that?"

There were only mumblings that quickly faded to silence at the surprise of being asked a question unexpectedly.

"The question, ladies and gentleman—the question." Again Michael drifted into his Darth Vader impersonation. "You will never know the power of the smart side, until you master the energy of the sales force, my young apprentices." Then he continued normally. "Which question is the question? The question that we should question, or rather that we should ask, is when? When were they planning to use our product or service? Their answer will eliminate the need to handle this objection later on. Again, we can link this angle nicely with the 'need to think about it' solution. I'll come back to that point later.

"The next point we come to is ... let's see here ... Number three, commitment. That's easily enough dealt with, because we can ask, 'How committed are you to having this product or service?' Using a reversal also works well here, if we were to ask prospects how they would feel not having our product or service. Perhaps it's how they'd feel having passed up the deal of the year.

"Marketing plays a great role in reversal-type sales–telling people what they 'must have' before they are even aware of it. The health and beauty industry is one great example because it uses fear in its marketing campaigns like no other. They sell people that they are ugly, unpopular, and stupid if they aren't a size two with perfect skin and style. Whether it be beauty products to clear up blemishes, clothing to hide the little extra weight that the holidays have added, or a weight-loss program to get them to their 'ideal' weight (and who dictates that?), our products will make them 'gorgeous.'

"The luxury industry is another. Take a look at cars, for example. Automobiles have never been sexier, more fun loving, and cooler than advertisements portray them now. What, are we driving? Herbie? Citroen even boasts of 'auto-emoçion.' What is that, anyway? Anyone here's car get 'emoçionelle' when the tank is low? Audi would have us believe the A6 is actually a black widow spider that is some sort of transformer that can climb around tunnel walls to overtake another vehicle. I'd challenge anyone to try that with my Audi. I gotta tell you, if my A6 starts spinning a web in my garage, I'm arming myself with bug spray and calling the exterminator—or the Terminator!"

A few chortles broke out, and one man seemed to be gasping for air from laughing so hard.

"Mini Cooper would have us believe their car is the most fun to drive, so much so that my girlfriend might lock me out of the car and take off in it. Well, that says enough for me—I'm not buying a Mini.

"Speaking of possible objections of either spouses or business partners, how do customers feel about them making the purchase? Do they trust their judgment, or will they need to confirm with others first? Often it's a cop-out. Business representatives love to use this one by saying they'll have to run it by their boss, their superior, Lord Vader, whoever. It's best to get it out of the way before it comes up. Simply ask customers how their spouse or partner feels about them in this endeavor, and your job's done! They can't bring it up again, because they've already told us whether they're fine with it. If there is any need to check with someone else, back off and reschedule for a time that the decision maker can be there.

"There are other commercials that would have us believe dolphins drive their cars happily through the ocean and playfully breach the surface in pods. When they get closer to the mainland, they can surf giant waves and bail out of the car. I'm guessing they've engaged cruise control until coasting safely ashore. I was raised thinking if I dreamed of swimming with dolphins, I was gay. What's this commercial getting at? Are their cars so much fun that they're gay to drive? I mean, come on, people! Are we really buying this?

"The answer is yes, people are. Perhaps not you and perhaps not me, but statistics show this type of marketing is working. For those brief moments we are entertained, the message is absolutely crystal-clear: 'Own and drive a Jaguar, and you'll be so gorgeous you won't be able to fight members of the opposite sex off with a stick!'"

Giggles and chuckles now arose into laughter across the room. As it died down, Michael continued. "Why is it so? Why do people buy into this stuff? The answer is irrelevant. There's an old saying that as long as enough people keep spooning it up, we'll keep shoveling it out, and there doesn't seem to be any end to the courses at the salad bar of idiocy. Remember this saying when you are planning your next marketing campaign: your marketing needs only be entertaining enough to get them in the door.

"Where were we? Oh yes, the final point. We come at last to our number-one objection. Many of you have been curious as to how we can navigate around the 'I need to think about it' condition. I've been to other seminars myself where sales gurus said that if this objection comes up, we haven't done our job properly as salespeople. I disagree, and their 'expert' advice doesn't help us when it does come up.

"The truth is it's one of the easiest to navigate around. We simply need to ask them directly, 'How long have you been thinking about this? What's gotten in the way of you doing something about this earlier? Is that still relevant?'

"Listen to their responses as actively as possible. Whatever their answer, our response has to link them back to the present moment. 'Then isn't it about time to get started? Then this came along at the right moment then, didn't it?' It is, after all, high time they made a decision. Today is a great day for deciding—as good as any other. Whether 'this' is you or the special offer you've got going on, the prospect needs to feel good in deciding to do something about the situation. The truth is that either way, he or she will be making a decision: to do, or to not do. How the prospect might feel if he or she chooses not to get on with it right away will depend on what type of person he or she is. Using DISC analysis, we can generalize that D and I types will respond well to the positive reinforcement of how great it will be to purchase, whereas S and C types will be more motivated by their fear of loss of not having made the purchase.

"Everyone's an individual and there will always be exceptions to the rule. These preclose guidelines are what have made the difference in my team closing 80–92 percent of all qualified prospects."

Preclose

Foreshadowing

Michael continued with his seminar. "Now, then, a quick recap of the preclosing guidelines we've been speaking about today.

"Number five: money, We'll be assured there is a budget before making it more reasonable for our prospects to make their purchasing decision. For an individual we might ask, 'Are you planning to use our product before or after work?' For businesses, we would be more apt to ask the representative of a company, 'About how much has your business budgeted for this?'

"Number four: time. We'll make sure it fits into their schedule and timetable. 'When were you planning to make use of our service? Is that realistic with your schedule?'

"Number three: commitment. Either way they're going to commit to something. We'll assist them however we can in staying committed to us. 'What do you want to do with our product after you've made your purchase?'

"Number two: spouse. We'll be assured it's okay with their spouse or business partner before we allow them to purchase. Are they in a position to make a purchasing decision, or does it depend on someone else? 'When can we all meet to go over everything together in more detail? They are sure to have their questions, which we'll be able to go over together before you make your decision.'

"And the number-one reason for saying no, 'I need to think about it,' can be intercepted simply by asking, 'How long is it that you've been thinking about this? What is it that you've been thinking about that's stopped you in the past? Is that still relevant?' After that, we can reassure them, 'There's no time like the present, then, is there?'

"By preclosing, we show both a genuine integrity and good business sense. We more actively play a role within the community, maintaining long-term business relationships by showing such integrity, and it shows that we plan to remain secure as a business for a long, long time. There is great truth to the old adage, 'People buy on emotion and justify with logic.' Preclosing helps people justify their purchasing decision when used correctly. A good salesperson navigates around potential problems before they come up, the same way a good driver navigates to avoid potholes."

After getting a signal from a woman on camera from one side of the stage, Michael checked his wrist. "I'm not into watches, and I'm being instructed that time does fly when you're having fun. I'm afraid that's about all the time we have for today. Those of you leaving us today, I wish you all a safe journey home and hope that you will choose to navigate your way back here tomorrow. Same time, same place! For those of you sticking around, I'll be in Harry's New York Bar to answer any questions you might have. Hopefully none of you will 'have to think about it,' and I will have the pleasure of your company there. It has been my pleasure speaking with you all. Good evening."

With that, a roaring applause rose up. Michael graciously absorbed it all and went through the crowd giving high-fives, shaking hands, and embracing people by the dozens. Though he wasn't able to get to everyone, he made a point of getting their attention, and sometimes a hand clapped on the shoulder with a sincere nod was enough.

After winking and smiling his way over to Jin and Steven, Michael leaned over to ask Steven, "Beer, or Kölsch?"

"Kölsch?" Jin replied, hearing the familiar sound.

Both Steven and Michael looked at each other and laughed as Steven chipped in, "It's decided! The Kölsch Brewery it is, my man!"

The exchange in German between Steven and Michael didn't help prepare Jin for what he was in for that night. He would have to rely on his martial arts training to steer him clear of getting into any potentially sticky situations.

Jin recalled the ABC martial arts philosophy recited when he went for his red-striped belt under Sensei Iura's supervision …

Balance and Flexibility
Red-Striped Belt

The ABCs of Conflict Avoidance:

A: Avoid any potentially dangerous situation.
B: Breathe; be calm if a situation appears to be going badly.
C: Communicate clearly, calmly, and with confidence.
D: Don't do anything that might make the situation worse.
E: Environment—use it to your advantage.
F: Fire: shout "Fire!" instead of "Help," to draw attention to yourself, if necessary.
G: Get away quickly, if at all possible.
H: Hit hard, hit fast, and hit first!

—Sensei Iura

Rules and regulations have always been there as guidelines for those studying martial arts; they are lessons taught during training to be helpful for avoiding violence as much as possible, but to be likewise prepared for that violence should the need arise. In general, the martial arts are about self-defense. But that raises the question of self-defense against what?

The principles of martial arts training are taught to be applicable in any situation. People nowadays are less likely to get into a brawl, as compared to the likelihood of the need to physically defend oneself during the times from whence they were developed. Still, those same principles can be applied in everyday situations from today's society for the modern-day warrior. The common person's fight to defend him or herself against poverty, abuse, hunger, and even against unhappiness are arguably equally valid now.

The nice thing is that all the principles are attainable by all people able to do just three things: look, listen, and think. Luckily, just about everybody can do them. The key is doing all three.

You want to survive crossing the street? Look, listen, and think! Try to cross the street by using only one of the steps—splat! Try to do it with two of the three—that's a one-in-three chance of splat!

You want good grades in school? Look, listen, and think! Pay attention to the teacher, listen to the teacher, and think about what the teacher is saying. You want to do well on your exams? Look, listen, and think! Read the question, hear it in your mind, and draw on the resources in your head to answer as best you can. That will eventually result in a better diploma, which will result in you having a better-paying job, which will result in more satisfying challenges in life.

Challenges met in the workplace are best met with a heightened sense of awareness, meaning nothing more than paying attention. Watching, listening carefully, and considering what is to be done will result in you making the right choices.

Try to learn, or to write an exam, or to do well in an interview for a job utilizing only one of the three senses, and you will fail. Using two of the three senses means the best possible result will be a one-in-three chance of failure—those are odds no gambler would take, so why should you?

There is a much lower chance you will get attacked or hurt during an attack if you are paying attention, listening, and thinking about what you are doing.

Buddhists sometimes refer to the eightfold path to enlightenment as a wheel that turns to reveal life's truths. The secret in unlocking each cog lies in one's awareness, or more simply put, phases where one was looking, listening, and thinking in balance and to the best of one's ability.

***

Jin observed how his martial arts training had prepared him to be prepared for any situation. Jin's red-striped-belt test had taught him beyond the lessons in physical self-defense. Jin looked beyond the classes developing his physical fitness, and he heard the rules about self-defense in his head, which went beyond his physical ability to defend himself. He realized the lessons learned were about governing all facets of his life with compassion.

And so it was that Jin's wheel turned an unusual direction on the other side of the globe.

During the conversation over diner, Jin was to learn more about the culture he was visiting. The Kölsch Brewery was the oldest in the city. Kölsch beer was by far the most popular beer to drink in Cologne, and it was one of the four features of the city that helped keep it independent from the rest of Germany. Cologne was widely regarded as a country within a country. Cologne was the media center of Germany (thus Media Park was built to encourage further developments), and it boasted waving the rainbow flag in acceptance more than any other city.

The local dialect spoken in Cologne was an old one known as Kölsch. It was not only so foreign as to require subtitles for the rest of the country, but their use of words and syntax seemed to be specifically designed to fool hopes of a smooth translation. Ordering a hen in a blanket will get you a slab of cheese with bread; it was known to the English as a plowman's lunch. Somehow, Cologne, or Köln, remained the richest city in Germany not founded by the Hansa pirates of old.

In any restaurant worth going to in Köln, locals may request a person known as a Kürbis (literally translated, a pumpkin), as opposed to a regular Kellner (waiter). Any complaints going to a Kürbis are likely to be met with total disregard, because, "Clearly, sir, you have requested to be served this way when you requested my services!" Unbelievably poor service was a sort of running joke that the locals seemed to find humorous. To understand the humor, one must be able to decipher the dialect; the bantering became more and more acceptable with each glass.

Allegedly, Kölsch, the beer, was best served cold in smaller-sized glasses, because it should never be around long enough to go stale; it's meant to be drunk quickly to enjoy the freshness. The 0.21 sized glasses mean the first glass or three could be tossed back as shots were often done in the States. When cold, one would never taste the 5.4 percent alcohol inside each glass. It was a wonder there weren't more alcoholics in Germany, but truth be known, Germans drank for pleasure, not to get drunk.

The Kölsch brewery sat around the corner from the marketplace at Cologne's majestic cathedral. The Kölner Dom was without question the fourth feature of the country within a country. Cologne's cathedral was regarded as the world's greatest Gothic structure ever known. Photos and postcards showed how hard both the city and cathedral were hit during the war. Its massive spires and hundreds of gargoyles were truly works of an architect's passion, in direct conflict with the structure's practicality. With some of the Dom's gothic detail due to fall, millions of tourists came here to view it each year. Its restoration was truly a monumental achievement.

What was oddly stirring was that the German people took no pride in the achievement. In fact, they took no great pride in any of their country's achievements, or in being German for that matter. In fact, it would seem the people held a residual shame about being born in Germany. Whereas Americans couldn't wait to weave the red, white, and blue into a conversation, Germans never spoke of their flag's colors, and most hung their heads and grew uneasily quiet at mention of the World Wars or Hitler. It would appear that post-war children were educated to be ashamed of their country; to shame themselves for what their forefathers had allowed to happen. The world disliked them for their being German, and the highest they could hope for was the respect of their fellow countrymen, never mind the notion of forgiveness of their neighbors. This respect could only be earned by working hard, keeping impeccable records, and maintaining punctuality as well as irrational edicts.

The sociological stress created by such a doctrine created an image of the German people as being cold and callous. Nothing could be further from the truth. Although initially cautious, the German people connected genuinely and wholeheartedly. Time and consideration were necessary before calling someone friend, because there were social responsibilities that were taken just as seriously as the grading of the autobahn.

Perhaps these characteristics of the German people were amplified for Jin, because he had now lived among the American people long enough to realize their initial super-friendliness was often without depth and lacked substance. Jin was amazed how men he'd spoken with back in the States spoke so viciously about women;

it appeared women were only interested in ripping off men for all their material wealth before ultimately degrading their social status to levels frustrating enough to either commit suicide or have an affair—either of which would be blamed on the male. It amazed him how these deranged views would carry a conversation to uncomfortable levels of how women were only to be used to please the man and then tossed away like rubbish. Then, literally a breath later, when their girlfriend would show up, the men would be nice as pie toward women, as if they were the angels of mercy themselves.

Deeper, truer convictions teemed at the marketplace square in Cologne, where true artists swam against the flows of a German restrictive society. They made art for art's sake and took great pride in each work, with no interest in timetables or punctuality. It was no wonder Cologne's Market Place Square was covered daily with drawings often worthy of a gallery. All was soon to be washed away when the next rain came.

It rained hard that evening. Tourists could wait it out comfortably either in their hotels or in expensive cafés, whereas the artists would eventually return to start again on the chalked renaissance works recently washed from the memories of the tourists and the square.

What would not wash so easily from Jin's memories of the trip was the rawness of the evening that ensued.

After a meal full of comical service, the comedy more easily understood by numerous droughts of beer, the three men were in high spirits by the time they headed off to the brewery. Laughing along the way, they traipsed their way over a rain-smeared portrait of Mozart.

"Do you know the rule of the road, Jin?" Michael asked.

Jin admittedly he did not, but Steven was kind enough to offer the answer. "What goes on the road, stays on the road, my man!"

Even in his inebriated state, Jin was able to appreciate the value of being included in this circle of trust, and no matter what antics were pursued during the evening, none would be held against them. It was an intimate bond. They would look out for each other.

They came upon the brewery door and were ushered in by a giant of a doorman, though others had to wait. "The big guy's a member at our club; I arrange the occasional massage treatment appointment for him, and I don't wait in line," Michael explained to his astute colleagues.

Hearing Michael's English, the doorman was seemingly pleased to have the opportunity to exercise his. "Would you gentlemens like a Kürbis?" he asked enthusiastically.

"No thanks, my good man," Steven replied. "We've already had dinner. Just send us some women when we order our third round, and if we want any more abuse, we'll take it from them!"

The doorman caught the gist of Steven's meaning and laughed heartedly. The large frame of the man seemed more jovial than intimidating. Even though his slap on Steven's back nearly took the man back half a step, there was a warmth to this person that made one comfortable knowing he was there should anything get out of hand.

What shocked Jin was when four girls came over to their table as they ordered their third round. The men raised their glasses and said, "Thank you." A quick glance around the room brought into sight the doorman, who nodded back with a grin. The three of them at the table looked at each other, and a smile became a roar of laughter before Michael could raise his glass with Steven and Jin to say, "Prost!"

"Cheers!" the girls answered back, suspecting the accents to mean that they were in good company and that the evening could continue in high spirit. There was a tempo of alcohol that flowed, and the small beer glasses never seemed to increase their level of intoxication but rather held it constant. Inhibitions melted from people who were not nearly as cold as propaganda would have Jin believe.

The Kölsch brewery was impeccably clean for a pub. Glasses were rapidly cleaned away when left on the table, which was also made of very thick glass so that patrons could see to the cellar below where the vats slowly brewed the beer they were consuming.

Kölsch beer was less expensive than Coca-Cola to purchase in Cologne. The refreshing taste of beer in Germany was protected by law; only certain water, barley, and hops could be used, and all ingredients were to be of the highest standard; testing was constant. German beer—that was to say, *genuine* German beer—couldn't be exported because it had no preservatives; they were illegal ingredients. As a consequence, beer had to be consumed within about two weeks of being brewed, and judging by the levels of consumption going on at the brewery, the people were making their best efforts to see that none went to waste. The level of fluids consumed meant bathroom breaks were regular, and there were usually one or two people absent from the table at any given time, depending on whether it was a guy or a girl who had to go.

When it was Jin's turn to go, he had a look around the brewery. The old, stained trusses looked darker against the white-painted stonework throughout the place. Although the place was relatively absent of color (even the waiters wore black and white), the room was full of flavor. People at the Kölsch brewery were out to have a good time and were doing just that. Across the smoke-filled room, which seemed to twist and turn before leading down some stairs to where the water closet could be found, everyone seemed to be greeting others warmly, as a friend not seen for some time.

Inside the restroom, Jin was confronted by a sloped, stainless-steel wall to wee on. The wall was designed with a constant stream of water that flowed evenly and gently away beneath the floor. The trickling water helped those unable to go.

It was commonplace in Europe for there not to be blinds, let alone individual stalls for men to maintain a level of privacy, as in Western culture. Jin stepped toward the wall, positioning himself between two strangers, and he pondered the good sense of the design; logically men were far less likely to miss their target, even after a few beers.

"Hey, you're pissing on the wrong wall," shouted someone, and a few heads including Jin's turned to see one gentleman having had somewhat more to drink tinkling away against the wall adjacent to the row of men.

Sometimes when there was nothing else to do about an ill situation, the only thing to do was laugh, and most of the men present did just that—not viciously, but in order to make light of the situation. No one seemed particularly upset by the man's actions.

A local commented in German toward the individual, boldly enough for any in the room to hear of the man's pending folly. This had two others laughing profusely, one of whom washed his hands of the matter and left.

The man who'd shouted was befriended to the man who'd lost his sense of direction. He continued to speak in what seemed a proper British accent. "Come on, then, just one more and it's time to go home, all right?"

Toilet? Jin had turned to read the sign outside and mused, *Why do Europeans call a restroom a toilet?* It was a question he would bring up upon his return to the group, and it should bring as much amusement as the girls' antics of why girls went together to the

WC. *For that matter, why is it a WC?* He chuckled to himself as his thoughts tinkled away.

Jin returned to the table to ask about why restrooms were called WCs. Steven looked very seriously at the group and explained without batting an eyelid, "It stands for 'Who Cares.'"

Jin grinned, and he thought to himself that with the antics to which he had been privy, there was an element of truth to the underlying meaning of Steven's predefinition.

Jin's thought was confirmed when one of the girls leaned over to him to look at him sincerely and casually stated, "I must piss." Jin nodded politely and watched her reach out her hand to the other girl sweetly and say, "Komm schon mit," to the other girl, so that she would tag along. As sweetly as she meant it, and as adorable as her accent was, German directness would take some getting used to.

"There they go, together. Why on earth do girls do that?" Steven brought up the topic from earlier, to stir up conversation anew.

"I imagine it's so one of them can point it out if the other ends up pissing on the wrong wall in the WC," Jin offered, and the mental imagery as well as Jin's choice of words had them in hysterics long enough to wait for the next round to arrive.

Michael had the answer. "Seriously, I understand WC stands for water closet. If I remember correctly, the term comes from the time when outhouses were first brought inside homes. They were the only rooms that had running water for all the purposes in the household, including filling the lavatory pots."

Michael paused for dramatic effect and had everyone guessing whether or not he was serious. Steven burst out laughing, and had everyone following his lead.

The girls at their table were originally from a small village outside the city of Bodrum, in Turkey; they were sisters, in fact. Meeting Turkish people in Cologne shouldn't have been too surprising, as Germans had long enjoyed holidays in Turkey. There was bound to be both immigration as well as emigration; exposure to one culture drove an interest in the other.

If these two were any indication of the women there, it wasn't difficult to imagine why they were kept out of sight as much as possible. Women in Turkey may very well be Aladdin's true treasure of the country. The girls' charm and alluring assets were enough for any single man to dream of a thousand and one nights spent with either of them. Their life's story read like a fairy tale: a Persian farmer for a father who sought only a life of peace for himself and his family. Marrying a Muslim girl for love, he adopted her religion for the sake of permission from her father to wed her. When he still didn't receive it, they took a great chance and ran away together to start a life of their own near the Aegean Sea. He proved to be a good provider and was never too short of love for any of their six children.

When the older of the girls was ten, her father brought home a television. It was a big deal for the family and changed their perspective on the world, because they were suddenly exposed to other cultures outside their own. Their clothing style, family values, and ritual beliefs were challenged. The oldest of the two sisters longed to experience the outside world for herself. Their father showed great compassion for her situation and agreed that much had changed in the world since he had knocked the green bottle off the roof of his wife's parents' house, placed there by her parents to indicate they had a daughter who was ready to wed.

Their father instilled in the girls high moral values and trusted their judgment and that they would do him no dishonor. It was for the girls' safety and security that he bid them to go together, so that no matter where they were, they would have each other.

Jin was surprised that the girls were drinking, thinking that was abhorred by the Muslim tradition. The younger sister explained that in a modern and much more liberal context, the Koran stated that being a good Muslim was not simply about praying five times a day and abstinence, but more about being a good person. Allah could forgive missing any amount of prayer or not abstaining, but it was clear that being a good Muslim meant being consistently compassionate toward others, as well as being a good person.

It was easy enough to see how one could follow all the rules and rituals and still not be a good Muslim. Jin saw that compassion wasn't limited to Buddhism, Christianity, or the Muslim faith. At their core, the religions were about being a good person. In essence, being a good Buddhist meant being a good Christian, which meant being a good Muslim.

Michael was able to see from downstairs that both the sisters were trim, as they had been sitting on the glass table whilst he'd been on his WC break; he'd noticed accidentally when he went to finish his glass and tipped it back to swallow. "Make no mistake about it, my friends," he said. "Both of those girls are for me!" They began to roar, and Steven even had a tear in his eye from laughing so hard.

The girls' return found the boys in good spirits, and that meant it was time to continue the party at another bar. Apparently Michael was well acquainted with the owner of a Persian bar, and they'd have no trouble getting in. The girls agreed to come along because apparently it was a really cool place to go.

Suite 54 was the hippest Persian club Cologne had to offer. The owner, Mr. Pfaraji, greeted them warmly at the door. They hadn't any trouble getting in after being subjected to Mr. Pfaraji's insistence and agreeing to call him by his first name, Pejman. The group was then escorted to a VIP section, and an enormous water pipe was set up for them with what they were told was apple-blossom flavor.

The place was luxurious. Every fabric was antiquely decorated in such an eclectic style that it seemed to go together. Giant, soft cushions lined the floor, which was cut away beneath the table so that one could comfortably sit at floor level.

Five gorgeous girls curled up to them, which was made easy by the cushions. Each of the beauties' deep, dark hair contrasted a bright smile. One laughed with wavy locks of hair, another with curled ringlets; two more had straight braided hair down their backs, and one had hers tied up tightly, making it impossible to tell how long her hair was.

Drinks flowed to the entire group. The water pipe, or *shisha*, was refilled. Jin had never smoked before, and his concern was laid to rest when Steven reassured him it wasn't drugs and was an experience he'd regret missing if he didn't try it.

Later, Jin would describe the experience to his cousin Art as unusual and cool. "You inhale deeply," he'd explain, "expecting to choke, but the experience is more like breathing in. There is neither a taste nor a feeling of filling the lungs with smoke. It's a breath like any other, except that you are very conscious of what you are doing. Just when you think you've done it wrong, you begin to exhale, and smoke starts to come out of your mouth or your nose, whichever you happen to be exhaling from at the time. And *then* you taste it—apple blossom. It's the weirdest thing!"

Strangely, it was a most comforting thing that Michael wouldn't allow anyone else to pay; he simply meant to be a great host. The three men felt like pashas, each with a harem and each without a care. The new company sprawled themselves all over them, hanging on every word they said.

They were having such a load of fun that it was surprising when Michael leaned over to mention the time. "Guys, it's five in the morning and I've got to be back in the office at seven. I'm taking these two sisters back home with me for a bit of, um, 'review.' The seminar starts at nine. Don't be late!"

With a smile, Michael was off with a sister on each arm. Steven and Jin would later hear just how Michael's night went.

Price Presentation

Neural-Associative-What?

8:30 AM

The wake-up call came through after what felt like all of twelve minutes of sleep, four of which were most likely spent tossing and turning. Jin answered the call because it was all Steven could do to wildly point at the phone and garble something that only cows had a chance to understand.

A cheery voice spoke pleasantly enough. "Good morning, my name is Annegret. Michael would be most grateful if you were able to meet him here at the club downstairs at nine o'clock." The friendliness of the voice was undeniable, perhaps somewhat wasted on the recipients this morning but undeniable. "We have arranged breakfast for you together. Thank you."

8:35 AM

Undeniably more effort was required in Jin's morning ritual calisthenics. Steven raised an eyebrow to discover Jin puffing away as the push-ups were completed.

8:58 AM

Showered, shaven, and yet somewhat ragged around the edges, Steven and Jin were greeted downstairs (although the route to get to the health club seemed to go down, over, and back up for no other purpose other than to befuddle hotel guests) by a hotel staff member. The same cheerful receptionist from the morning's wake-up call asked them to wait briefly on the couches across from the desk, which although unbelievably firm felt amazingly comfortable this morning. Jin chose to stand and learned from Annegret that Michael would be just a moment, because on his "late day," Michael started an hour later than usual, at 7:00 AM!

9:00 AM

It was the first time they'd be meeting Michael so early at his place of work. Both Steven and Jin expected Michael to be a little worse for wear just as they themselves were feeling. Yet, there before them was the quite stylish Michael Arneson in his role as regional sales manager of a major health club chain operating in Europe. His job was to ensure that the company hit some pretty aggressive sales targets, and as long as the individual clubs did so, the company left him to his devices.

Steven was working out about how many minutes of sleep his old friend had had or had neglected, but annoyingly, there were no signs of his being tired. It was oddly humorous to see Michael in his guise after the debauchery the night before, which didn't seem to fit in this environment.

Michael was in a three-piece suit, a definitive D-type characteristic. His walk and demeanor, although flamboyant, reflected directness at every turn. It was doubtful there could have been room for any caution in his character. And although there was a distinct firmness that projected from his attire, there was also a fairness underlying his character that showed in his eyes.

The staff, eager to practice their English skills, were there to ask how Steven and Jin had heard of Michael and were comfortable in mentioning his style of management as being firm, but fair.

9:03 AM

Michael whisked them away through the parking lot to the restaurant in the plaza. A table was reserved for them, and they were graciously seated.

"Steven, do you ever think how crazy it is what we get paid to do?" Steven nodded back at Michael's opening a topic for discussion as they were seated.

Seeing that Jin wasn't quite able to follow, Steven helped fill in the gaps. "You see, my man, Michael and I—and probably a lot of other people—get money from people for teaching other people how to get more money out of other people."

Michael added, "All Steven and I ever bring to the salespeople we train are the simplest of tools. It's kind of crazy."

"The crazy thing is that businesses continue to pay us as long as we continue convincing them—"

"Selling them," Michael corrected.

"Okay, selling them that we are required."

"One of the key to neuro-linguistic programming is in that justification factor."

Steven said, "We buy on emotion but justify with logic?"

"Yes, that's the one. So all Steven and I have been teaching for the last, I don't know, ten-plus years is how to artificially raise prices and then reduce them to arrive at the price they mean to sell their goods and services at."

"I used to call it the double discount system," Steven interjected with a grin at the memories of times when he and Michael worked together.

Michael elaborated. "It works like this. Say at our fitness center, we mean to sell memberships with a joining fee of 149 Euros and monthly dues of either 79 or 69 Euros, depending on whether people join for 12 or 18 months. All we do is tell each and every prospect, 'Our regular prices are a 249 joining fee and monthly dues of either 99 or 89.' Notice how we don't mention currency. Money has value; numbers do not. Even the programs we give names to refrain from a creating a sense of commitment. Telephone companies do it all the time: they advertise their 'friends' or 'home' packages."

Steven commented, "They are the kings of package sales, that's for sure. Even the words they use to name their eighteen- or twenty-four-month packages are carefully selected to create images of trust."

"It's not unique to their industry, though," Steven noted. "We've used 'friends' as a deal for when two people or more joined at once, and it worked fine. Back to the point. We then tell our prospects: 'There's a sale on now where you can save fifty Euros off their joining fee and ten Euros from their monthly dues, regardless of which program they subscribe to.' Sellers should ask if customers have a general preference for either this or that program."

Michael said, "Heck, my man, we used to even leave the pen hanging on the program we earned the most commission from, or the one we meant to sell the most of to hit company targets, just to influence their choice that little bit extra!"

"As absurd as it sounds, it's true," Steven admitted. "It's in the little things that never get noticed but that can influence prospects ever so slightly to choose one of the two options before them. The worst-case scenario was that they bought the cheaper option, but a sale would still be made."

"The real key to closing a deal is your ability to know when to shut up …" Michael started

"And just present two options for buying, either this one or that one, and shut up," Steven completed.

"Shut up and wait for them to speak. The only words they can say are either this or that, and either one of those are purchases. If you speak first, you'll have blown it. You'll have given them a reasonable excuse to need to think about it some more," Michael suggested.

Thinking about it carefully, Jin could now remember that both Steffi and Matt doing exactly that. Jin's failing was that he had often spoken out, perhaps too soon.

Steven watched the wheels turning in Jin's expression before mentioning, "Many salespeople talk about having the gift of the gab, but the best salespeople have an ever-present ear. It can be uncomfortable, even nerve-racking, to remain silent and wait. There have been times when I could feel a bead of sweat roll down my forehead from the pressure."

Michael jumped in to remind Jin, "If you are feeling the pressure, chances are the prospect is feeling it too. The difference is that you know where that pressure is coming from, so try to take comfort in that and relax."

Steven broke in to the conversation. "After all, you're not ripping them off. You're simply presenting them a price if they choose to buy right then and there. That's the necessary justification factor taken care of; the sale sorts itself out, provided you've created enough emotional connections for the prospect on all the other points."

Michael described the situation in the health club. "We present our prices in a way that encourages our prospects to purchase our services right away. We offer them a reason to buy. Monetary discounts are logical reasons that work. That's why many store windows say 'sale' or 'save.' That type of first impression will draw people into their business. A sign isn't terribly personal, so personalities are required.

"Salespeople's personalities provide the human element that makes the process more enjoyable. One person can't get along with absolutely everyone, which makes room for different people to become great at selling. Everyone does it anyway, and any one of those people can do it better. Businesses hire personalities willing to try."

Over the remainder of breakfast they discussed the planning of the day. Michael was a self-proclaimed control freak and functioned best when he knew where all the pieces were supposed to be. They would meet after the seminar for dinner and drinks. Michael had made reservations at Media Park. There would be a party for a group known in Cologne as the Golden Boys in the tower afterward.

Breakfast at the Plaza was laid out with such excellence in service as to provide luxurious taste and experience. Smoked salmon adorned by paper-thin sliced red onions was presented on freshly baked bread, with a tablespoon of cracked pepper–marinated olive oil drizzled over. Mineral water and fresh fruits from the morning's marketplace were also served. Orange juice was pressed to order, and European-strength cappuccinos were served to complete the meal. It was the perfect breakfast to erase the sluggishness caused by a lack of sleep from the night before.

Jin thought topick up the tab as a gesture of thanks for Michael's hospitality and Steven's including him on this trip. Also, Jin was feeling a little guilty for Michael always picking up the tab. The bill was served, and it was apparent that Cologne was an incredibly expensive city.

Michael stopped Jin as he offered to pay by explaining to Jin, "You are my guests and my friends. I would never invite you somewhere and expect you to pay. I would consider it discourteous! Please, my friends, let me take care of you and ensure that you are comfortable.

You have traveled such a great distance to see me, for which I am grateful. Allow me this small gesture of thanks."

Jin concurred with the sincerest thanks he could in English. It was so much easier in Japanese to show the right level of gratuity and respect—there are nine different levels of saying, "Thank you." The highest level was reserved by ancient Samurai warriors for their emperor. English, with its largest vocabulary in the world, still had room to expand in the area of meaningful expression.

Jin explained the predicament that he found himself in to both Michael and Steven, in that he would've liked to have expressed a somewhat greater level of thanks for all Michael's kindness and generosity, but the English language, unfortunately, didn't allow him to do so. Michael patiently listened to the complexity of what he took to be the simplest of matters (i.e., saying a thank-you and moving on) before responding in kind. "I appreciate your gesture, Jin, but let's look at this logically. Have you done the math on this seminar thing? I think I've got two hundred and fifty people in that hall. Each of them is paying four hundred Euros a pop to be there. How much is that?" Steven was about to say somewhere in the neighborhood of ten thousand when Michael recalled suddenly, "*And* I'm getting the room for free from the hotel manager; he wants a staff discount at our club. He'll probably get it … maybe." His smile caused them all to laugh, Steven the most heartedly of the group. "Anyway, it added value to my credibility to be able to say, 'People are flying in from all over the world to hear this seminar, so be there!' I probably got an additional twenty sign-ups just because of that, so don't worry about it. I'll gladly get the bills."

It was nearly time to get started on day two of the seminar.

Michael told them, "Time to take our places. Guys, enjoy the show!"

Close

This or That?

After seating themselves in a slightly different location, Steven and Jin were able to get not only a different vantage point, but they were better located to hear any potential comments from others in the crowd.

Switching stances back and forth from right, to center, and then to left profile, Michael began the seminar under the limelight with the simplest of questions. "Does this tie make me look fat?"

The crowd's laughter meant that the ice was successfully broken. *Some people have a knack for it,* thought Jin, *others don't. However, though anyone can potentially cultivate it, not everyone does.*

"Those of you who know me know about how I came over here with about four hundred Euros in my pocket and no job. How much was the entrance fee for this seminar, by the way?" There was a pause as mumblings and revelations revealed a similar amount was being asked. "Really? About four hundred, you say? Per person?" He was half-inquisitive with a raised eyebrow, followed by an enthusiastic grin "Wow, I've done pretty well here this weekend! The price of the seminar today—coincidence, d'ya think? I doubt it. My point is, don't undersell whatever service you are offering. If it's good enough for them, chances are it's good enough for someone they know. Ask for the referral, and you will receive it. Do it well, but do it. Not asking will guarantee you a very sound result as well."

Looking through his thumb and forefinger much like a spyglass to drive the point home, Michael added, "Nada, nix, niente, null. Which do you want? Ultimately people want to make up their own minds about everything. They are most likely emotional about their decision to buy whatever it is they are thinking about buying. Again, we buy on emotion and justify with logic.

"As salespeople, we just present them with a reason to buy. Whether or not we're using neuro-linguistic programming to raise their awareness, people often need to have their purchasing decision justified externally. That's where the ear of a good salesperson comes in. I'd like to think that to be a great ear for people, and therefore a great salesperson, we can raise that skill to neuro-associative conditioning. I was going to assume that everyone here knows aboutneuro-linguistic programming, but as my grade-six teacher from Liverpool said to me when you assume …" Michael wrote the word on the overhead projector, He then circled both the first three and the last two letters before stating, "You make an 'ass' out of 'u' and 'me.' So let's review quickly.

"Some sales gurus out there would con you to believe there's some sort of mysticism about neuro-linguistic programming, or NLP for short, and that companies need to pay oodles of cash for seminars delving deeply into its mystery. Hands up—who likes saving money?" There were various nods and a few hands that rose. "C'mon, who would like to save oodles of cash right now?" A much louder portion of the audience agreed they were interested to do so. Then, once Michael had their undivided attention, he made a pondering pause and scratched his head as if he had a question. "How much is oodles?"

Michael's whiplash smile impacted the crowd with a tempered level of comic relief.

"Well, I don't know how much oodles is, but it sounds like it has a lot of Os! I don't know about you, but I am *always* interested in saving those Os. I'm going to save you those oodles of cash right now by stating the blatantly obvious: that NLP is nothing more than offering people a choice between this or that option. Would you like this or that? Would you like that one or this one? Which option suits you better, this or that?

"If the prospect has any remaining objections, we isolate, reiterate, and feed them back to them with a clincher to purchase our product or service right away. We change their objection to a condition."

Michael framed each letter in the air with his hands as he spoke. "That's all there is to NLP! If you don't get it"—he repeated the framing process—"you're 'Not Listening Properly!' So, save yourselves from hiring some guru to come along and charge you oodles for what you already know. For any sales consultants out there now who are looking for an edge in their next gig, don't mind what I'm saying—after all, there are still a number of prospects who haven't attended this seminar weekend. I'm not denying the value of a refresher sales course. Repetition, a different point of view, and the same lessons coming from different sources are great learning-enhancing methods. My challenge to you is to be original in your approach. Be true to yourself, and that will be enough."

Michael went on to describe the leading process used in NLP, giving examples on each of the five objections, four of which could be summarized with the following scenario:

> "So, just so I understand you correctly, and I think that I am, the only thing holding you back from making your purchase decision today is … [the cost? the time involved? the length of the commitment? that you need to think about? that you need to check with someone else?)]"
>
> Wait for a nod and then continue to say, "If there was some way I could [reduce the cost? fit the time involved into

> your schedule? reduce the length of the commitment? find out and solve whatever it is that you need to think about it? enable you to check with someone else?], we could get started on this right away. Is that right?'
>
> Wait for a yes and then continue to say, "I'm going to run that by my [manager, senior advisor, whatever]. Let me see what I can do for you. I'll be right back.'" Then simply get up and go somewhere else for two minutes.

Michael went on to joke about the times when he had no senior advisor and had to grab any old employee who happened to be around in plain view (but out of earshot). He'd ask that person if they'd watched television last night, to which the person would shake their head no. Then he'd compliment the person on their contribution as a member of the team, thank him or her, shake their hand, and explain that he had to get back to a customer but would catch up with him or her soon, to which he or she would usually nod yes.

Michael would come over to the client and say how he didn't think the manager would go for it, but he did, and then he'd simply close the deal. Sometimes he'd be the senior advisor for his teammates, and five minutes later they'd be his.

No coworkers available? Not a problem! He'd go in his office and call either a girlfriend or an old friend, or make a date, or catch up quickly with family before returning to his prospect and claiming the same thing.

"Just fake it till you make it!" was the general rule. The manager's close was nothing more than offering a second opinion from a controlled source—namely, one he had control over, like a member of the staff.

If Michael was at all tired from the previous evenings, Jin saw nothing of it. Signs of perspiration were easily attributed to either the bright spotlights that Michael was working under or the intensity with which he was working.

Michael had previously decided to film the entire seminar, to market and sell later; this way he could reach out and share his knowledge with more people. There was no room for mistakes, and no one could deny he was putting everything into this weekend. The pressure Michael was under was as immense as the knowledge base he shared.

"Good sales figures or closing ratios are a matter of good showmanship and listening skills. Know the parameters of what you can and cannot do, but the rest comes down to showmanship. Everybody likes getting a deal, so give everybody one; that will entice more referrals to your business and generate more sales in a way that is more difficult to measure but equally important."

This was the start of neuro-associative conditioning, for which Michael wrote on the projector screen, "NAC."

"However, having great sales figures or great sales-closing ratios are about creating a purchasing community or environment, and I'm going to explain how to do just that. We're going to build on what it takes to be a good salesperson—that is, the active listening process, the mirroring of body language, intonation, all that stuff. But don't let it end there, ladies and gentlemen! Just as we should never stop recruiting—and some would add, we should never stop applying ourselves—consider that these elements are only the beginning. Are they important? Of course! But if we're to take salesmanship to the next level; if we're to create a purchasing culture around our business; if we progressively mean to reach out into our potential market viscerally, then we're going to need a much more solid foundation. Like any foundation, these elements need to be secure before we build on them.

"Remember that very little is communicated verbally; the rest is communicated with body language. There are studies that will tell you that only 11 percent of all communication occurs verbally; others claim only 7 percent. And look here." Michael held up a newspaper. "Last week's *Die Welt* claims it's 9 percent. Ladies and gentlemen, it doesn't matter if it's actually seven, nine, or eleven. We can associate the differences in the results as being indicative of our individuality. Some people communicate verbally more clearly, while some listen better than others ... as every married woman knows." Female laughter broke the silence of Michael's pause.

"To which," Michael added, "I'll wager every man out there wishes women would simply say what they mean." Numerous mumbled "Mmm hmms" were made under breath throughout the room by the male contingent. One or three met with a light smack on the arm by their female counterparts, for being so cheeky. Still, everyone smiled at the anti-revelation.

"Isn't it interesting that with languages having evolved as much as they have, we still rely on body language and the 'how they said it' factor so heavily. Once we acknowledge that most of our communication is done physically, we can use it to our advantage.

"The foundations of mastering the sales process lie in how well we can listen. Are we passively listening, or are we actively listening? We all feel the difference inside of us when we phone pretty much any customer-service line to ask something important to us, and they're on the phone going, 'Uh-huh ... yup ... oh, uh ... uh-huh.' You want to tear their heads off! Or is that just me? That's visceral! That's what I'm talking about here, albeit an example of reaching people in a negative sense. It illustrates my point exactly. Imagine the effect on your business of reaching people viscerally in a positive way and on a regular basis.

"There's a wise story about a troubled prince as he approaches the age of marriage. The young prince hears of a yogi who 'knows all in the world.' He leaves the palace grounds to seek him out and learn whom he should marry.

"As the prince is climbing the mountain on which the yogi is said to live, the prince comes upon an injured peasant woman. The woman fell from attempting the climb herself. The prince carries the woman up the mountain to the yogi for help, where he asks, 'Who is the most important person in my life?'

"The woman falls into unconsciousness from her injuries, and the yogi responds by asking the man to help him fetch and prepare some firewood to keep the woman warm. The prince is a kind young man and agrees to help. Even when a storm comes, the prince honorably fetches, cuts, and prepares firewood for the wizened man. The yogi speaks no word to the prince. The prince reasons he is searching for the answer.

"After four days, having only his sword with which to cut the wood, the young prince lays an abundance of firewood close to the yogi's home so that he may access it easily. He asks the yogi again, 'Who is the most important person in my life?'

"The yogi answers, 'My food stores are now low, and the storm has torn my garden apart. Will you not help an old man so that he will not starve?'

"The prince resows the garden so that the old man may heartily feast through the winter to come. After two days digging in the rocky mountain soil with his scabbard, the royal seal of his sword is barely recognizable. The prince works very hard to complete the task just as winter arrives.

"Again the prince's thoughts turn to his quest. 'Kind sir, will you not tell me who is the most important in my life?'

"The yogi responds, 'My cave is too barren. Will you not help me gather grasses and leaves, that this woman might have a softer place to rest?'

"When the peasant woman awakens the next day, she finds herself safe and secure in the yogi's cave on a soft bed of dried grasses and leaves. She owes her life to the men before her. The yogi's healing skills were successful in healing her injuries while the prince took care of them both to make every comfort available.

"The prince came to question the yogi a final time. 'Please, tell me now, who is the most important person in my life?'

The yogi responded, 'The answer is before you always.'

"As the day passed, the prince pondered the meaning of the words. It was midday when the woman came to speak. 'I must return. Might I have your coat, to stay the cold of the nightfall when I return with thanks from my village?'

"The prince, not having reached any conclusion as yet, offers his own vestments and sword, should she need to make her step more stable. The woman returns with breads and furs for the both of them late that evening. In the morning she speaks to them. 'My lords, I give thanks for all that you have done for me and beg forgiveness for the scarcity of these offerings. But I would tell of another truth that will offer greater thanks, great prince. I immediately recognized the seal on your vestments as well as your sword. In truth, I was your enemy—an assassin who hid on this mountain once our scouts received word that you sought the advice of a great yogi. But for my fall, you would not have needed to carry me, yet carry me you did. You, a prince, who treated me with respect and as an equal; you, who took care of me no less than one would a loved one. I return now to tell you that I have informed our troops of your humble and kind ways, and that no sword shall be raised against such a noble man.'

"The prince, stunned by the woman's story, turned to the yogi. 'How can it be that the answer is before me and yet eludes me so?'

"The yogi replied, 'But your question is answered. Had you not carried this woman to me, your enemy's troops would have come through the mountain and slaughtered you. But for your kindness to her, she would have tried to assassinate you once more, and perhaps succeeded. Had you not humbly helped me with firewood for my cave, we might all have frozen, and your armies would be at war. Not to mention that your patience and self-determination to understand my words caused you to stay in the safety of the mountains, away from your enemies (who knew naught of your deeds), which allowed you to live long enough to gain the wisdom you sought. The person in front of you is the most important person in your life. How you treat people, how you act around them, and how you hold yourself will determine the outcome of every encounter.'"

As Michael allowed time for the moral of the story to sink in, he sighed. A long look of contentment crossed over his face that Jin could easily see from his vantage point.

"The person in front of you is the most important person in your life. How simple and wonderful a philosophy! Whether it be your friend or your enemy, treat people well and be genuine to yourself, and you will succeed! What I am suggesting to you today, ladies and gentlemen, is not the impossible."

Michael cleared his throat, paused and continued in a most serious voice. "Your mission, should you decide to accept it, is to go beyond actively listening, look the person in the eye, and care. It is not beyond the ability of anyone in this room. It is not dependent on age, sex, religion, or creed. All I mean for you to do is interact with others on the most sincere level you can. Utilize the time available to talk about what brought them to you, as opposed to performing a survey of questions. Be there to discover their actual needs and then provide two options for them, 'Either this or that option.'

"Whether or not they purchase then, you've won. If they decide not to purchase, be understanding that now is not the right time for them but that when their situation changes, your business will still be there for them. That person can say no ill of you or your business. People remember how well they are treated, not whether or not they purchased. This goes beyond treating people professionally. We have to treat people well—not just once in a while, but all of the time, at every opportunity. That goes for both inside and outside your business.

"By being a genuinely good person, you will be shaping the way people perceive you, how they trust you. Who doesn't want to be known as a good person? As honest? As a positive member of the community? And that, ladies and gentlemen, is where we begin to create a cultural perception. We reach out into our community and we create attitudes and perceptions We sculpt a culture of people more willing to make purchases. We raise their acceptance of salespeople in their community and thereby create an environment where they are more likely to purchase because of their subtly (dare I say, subconsciously) raised emotional state.

"People buy based on their emotional state. I say to you now that often—not all the time, but often enough—the opportunity is there to lower the emotional threshold required on a more universal level. That way, the emotional state of the average individual doesn't need to be raised as much. And, as long as we're raising their emotional state just a little more than our competition is, we will reap the rewards! By being the founder of their cultural acceptance, they will be more likely to justify the logic of purchasing your product and/or services!

"Like the horse that wins the Triple Crown at Ascot, the UK's most prestigious raceway, we only need be better by a nose to win. There are no wreaths for the horse that places second; there are no half-a-million-pound rewards for the owner of the second-place thoroughbred; no one remembers the name of the jockey who rode to second place (otherwise known as first place of all the other losers). There is no promotion for a job well done to the horse master of a second-place horse."

Michael paused for a drink of water. After reasserting himself, he straightened his posture with a renewed energy one might call a second wind before continuing. Second wind? It was difficult to say how many winds Michael had had to suck up over the course of the weekend, let alone which wind this one represented.

Referrals

The Three Rs

Michael continued his seminar. "There are three rules to reaping your repeat business, and they all begin with the letter R." He wrote three Rs vertically lined up on the overhead screen. Michael spoke as he clarified their meaning for everyone in attendance, reaching out as if to shake people's hands.

"Referrals, referrals, and referrals."

Turning on his heel to allow the crowd to follow his lead, Michael continued.

"Marketing analysts would have us believe that, statistically, it cost us 15 percent of the value of our product (no matter what our product or service is) to acquire a new client through standard marketing techniques. However, those same analysts would have us believe it only cost 15 percent of *that* to acquire a new client through a referral system. Whether or not the numbers are exact, I believe it's safe to assume it costs a lot less to acquire a cold client than it does to acquire a warm one.

"It's no secret that times are tough. That's a given, because competition is greater than ever before, and it will continue to grow. We all want more and more clients. Passive referrals aren't enough of a basis on which to plan business growth, because it's impossible to know where they are coming from and at what frequency or magnitude they will come. Active referrals should be part of your business planning and will allow you to have some idea as to from where future business is coming.

"How do you get them, you ask! The more you ask, the more you get. It's as simple as that. So ask as much as you can, and then ask again."

Michael wrote out the word "Referral" on the screen for everyone to see. Before continuing, he picked up the glass of water and held it casually. "Anyone here know a competitor who seems to invest little time and money into marketing and yet reaps the rewards of all your hard work? Perhaps a work colleague who seems to do very little and yet rises quickly within a company? No? Must just be me, then." He smirked behind the glass as he had a sip of water and then set it down. Michael's point was made.

"We all know people like this, and it may be that it sickens you how this can be. But I would recommend you look, listen, and learn from them, because most likely they have some highly developed personal skills that allow them to build strong relationships that they can leverage into more and more business or promotion. What works for them may not work for you, though. Everyone has his or her own style, and I invite you to allow yours to develop. To do that, we need to understand what a referral is."

Clearing his throat and straightening up his posture in a quite pompous manner, Michael bastardized an English accent and seemed to be quoting *Webster's Dictionary*. "A referral is a warm lead generation system that takes advantage of people's inherent desire to help." Reverting back to his natural tone, Michael reiterated, "An inherent desire, ladies and gentlemen. We all have an inherent desire to help one another. Remember those analysts we were speaking about? They would conclude that the anecdotal evidence suggests more than half the people you know would be willing to recommend others to you, and around one-third of the names produced would result in new business. Those clever little bean counters know something about everything. What is that for a title anyways? Anal-ist? All those numbers and statistics, only to reach the conclusion that the results are inconclusive and that they are at best left open for interpretation. The constant revisions and charts get a bit extreme for my taste at times—more like anal lists, if you ask me."

Chuckles rose and Michael anchored the room firmly by preframing the next part of the seminar.

"There are only two major factors that could be holding you back from generating referrals. Either you are not asking, or you are not asking very well. It takes a certain type of courage to ask for a referral. So ask courageous questions! It may seem daunting, but I intend to give you all an 'easy out' method of asking, just for attending here today.

"Just as we all know not to ask, 'Can I help you,' but rather 'How can I help you,' the key to asking for referrals is much the same. How many times have you asked, 'Do you know someone who …' whatever? The easy out is to ask, 'Who do you know who …?' It's an easy out for your client, not for you. It's an open-ended question that won't make him or her feel pressured or intimidated to come up with the names of a person or three who might also … whatever.

"If clients can't, give them an escape route so as not to make them feel uncomfortable. If they don't have names and numbers they are willing to part with, understandingly tell them, 'Listen, there's no need to think of anybody right now. If you can give it some thought, we can come back to it later.' Ideally, within a week's time."

Michael went on to describe how this was a very powerful yet natural position to be in. Health insurance salespeople were perhaps the best at creating this type of pressure. "There are insurance companies out there that require as many as nineteen names and numbers for their giving you a discounted rate on your insurance package. Nineteen! That's the kind of high-pressure sales that give salespeople a bad name! A bit of honest preframing can go a long way for you when generating great referrals. Be as direct as you are honest when asking. For example, start with, 'I wonder if you could help me. We're trying to grow our business at the moment. We're in the process of updating our mailing lists and only want to send the information to people who might be interested. I'm looking for a project just like this one. I'm trying to build my portfolio.'

"A compliment doesn't do you any harm, either. Something light and along the lines of, 'I get the feeling you come across quite a lot of people. Seems to me you have some pretty strong connections. You seem to be the person to know in your business.' And then go directly for the close: 'Who do you know who would …?'

"We're going to break for a brief intermission before we return for a bonus section of the weekend titled 'Mastering the Sale.' Before we do, I'd like to suggest that sales aren't unlike sparring in a boxing ring. We need to be sure of our footing and know a few moves before we get in the ring. Like a boxer, we need to assess our position. Positioning is everything—as my girlfriend keeps reminding me—so practice moving with ease and with your guard up. Nice and easy, bob and weave. Keep it natural until you feel the rhythm. Keep your form relaxed until you spot an opening, and then boom! Go for the throat and fill your bucket with fresh, warm, referral blood! Ding!"

Michael's boxing ringside imitation cued the lights to allow participants an opportunity to freshen up before returning to learn about mastery.

After the break, Michael jumped right back into the lecture as if he hadn't missed a beat. "What does it take to master a sale? It takes applying our efforts the right way. Applying ourselves is a prerequisite for the other principles of the path toward mastering the sale. Without the right effort, nothing can be achieved. We've all probably experienced how misguided effort or spreading ourselves too thin distracted us from some task or another in the past, and confusion set in. Or is that just me?"

Michael paused for a drink of water from a glass that had reappeared at the side of the stage. "No one here ever felt spread too thin? Surely you, sir?" He pointed randomly into the crowd roughly toward a distinctively enormous gentleman. The gentleman nodded as he adjusted his position in his chair in order to more dramatically tap his large waistline, and he smiled back at Michael.

"Anyone else?" he let the words linger with a subtle humor that anchored the crowd to him, and though Michael only pointed in one direction, it was as though everyone was met by his hand's accusation, and they involuntarily nodded and mumbled some form of concurrence before Michael continued on a more serious note. "Our mental energy is the force behind the right effort; it occurs in either wholesome or unwholesome states. It is the same type of energy that fuels desire, envy, aggression, and violence. That mental energy can fuel self-discipline, honesty, benevolence, and kindness. We are in control of our aptitudes and therefore can influence our outcome if we simply govern them to be wholesome and catch ourselves as much as possible before the unwholesome ones can take root.

"Consciously it involves effort—mental self-discipline. It's not easy to prevent the arising of unwholesome states we aren't even aware exist within us; it takes effort to let go of unwholesome states that already are nearly part of our character. But these things are necessary if we are to make room for more wholesome states to occur within us and then maintain and perfect those wholesome states once they've arisen.

"The good news is that positive mental states are addictive—more addictive than any drug, and more enjoyable ... Maybe not as enjoyable as sex, but I can tell you it will make sex more enjoyable. More than anything, it feels good to like yourself for the person you are. It all starts with how you think, so learn to govern it. Sure, you'll screw up once in a while, but don't panic. Set yourself back on the wagon, and you'll get there. Your thoughts will turn to words. Your words will turn to actions. Your actions will turn to traits. Your traits will become your character, and your character will influence your success as much as the amount of pleasure you extract from your life.

"These are the foundations of what it takes to master a sale. Being a good salesperson is about being a good person. Notice how the word 'person' is even there to remind you of this. Being a great salesperson is about being a great person, so as you can no doubt deduce, mastering the sales process is about mastering your person. Where does it go after the foundations are laid?"

Michael went on to describe the framework of mastering the sales process. So began the builder's analogy, with a picture of a house that looked like a four-year-old drew on the screen above him. The principles should be simple enough that a four-year-old should be able to follow it, so Michael claimed to keep the image as simple as possible. He stated, for the record, that it had absolutely nothing to do with the fact that he couldn't draw.

"The framework of sales lies in acceptance that we are all different and all equal at the same time. That as people, no matter what our beliefs, language, culture, creed, or sexual orientation, we have needs and would like to be treated respectfully. All belief systems, languages, and cultures, go beyond the color of our skin and orientation at their roots to deliver the same message: 'If you want to be treated nicely, treat others nicely. If you want to be treated with respect, treat others respectfully.'"

Michael went on to describe how all incidents of violence might be attributed to misinterpretation, misguidance, or persons being misled away from the human race's highest virtues. "So, do the opposite of creating catastrophe in order to create the opposite result. Listen and treat others well. Be good enough so that if you were your client, you'd want to give you a referral. Be so damn good that people rave about you and tell stories about you to whoever will listen."

During this lecture, Jin could imagine his mother saying, "Differences in opinion are seeds of opportunity to the person with a compassionate heart." She was always such an inclusive person, listening and treating all Jin's friends so wonderfully that his friends would rather play at his house than at any other. Jin's trip down memory lane was interrupted by the power in Michael's voice as he went on.

"The finishing work," Michael said as his builder's analogy of mastering the sales process drew to an end, "was in the fine-tuning of the self to be compassionate toward the needs and desires of other people—all others, without exception. Language differences are only there to stretch our vocabulary, and cultural differences are amazing opportunities to increase the understanding of no less than ourselves. The human race *is* a race, ladies and gentlemen. As with any race, the position we'd like to be in is out there in front, leading the way. To be that person, one has to lead by example and hold on to one's convictions whenever they are challenged. And they *will* be challenged ... and then ridiculed ... and then eventually held for obvious truth.

"I invite you to walk away if someone doesn't show you the respect you desire, unless you feel the opportunity is there to learn something of another person's perspective and increase your understanding of another's needs. With that, we master sales. This is a far greater journey than many of you have opted for, but know that it is not beyond anyone's reach and that the principles I talk about here are universal for any job. A job is just a job. Teaching you something to do your job better has a value for sure. You will benefit from such teachings for as long as you have the job. But teaching you how to bring love into your job no matter what your job is—that's something that you can benefit from for life.

"We can all become sales masters; everyone can." Michael glanced round the room, and Jin couldn't be sure if he had picked Steven and himself out among the crowd as he glanced over in their direction. As he did so, Michael began another analogy. "Or better yet; we can all become samurai of the sales front. These modern-day warriors are the most desirable assets among the corporate battlefield." Michael smiled at the newfound catch phrase. "Samurai salespeople or not, ladies and gentlemen. The choice is yours. What do you want to be?

"Good? Just getting on with your job as one would just get on with one's lives? I think everyone in this room wants more, or you wouldn't be listening to me right now …

"Perhaps you mean to be great, performing your job better than the rest? This will no doubt bring you much job satisfaction, but is your position or business secure enough to endure a bad month or three?

"So, how about guru? Extending the life of your current career or business, whatever it may be, by preaching practices to others? Telling others what to do (and getting paid for your opinion, which is fun in itself) allows responsibility to fall to someone else to bring in better results. Whether you're a consultant, a manager, or a business owner, people will always argue that it was your knowledge shared that brought in their results.

"But what about being a samurai, living your life fully and thereby influencing those around you without the need to preach, as they will model themselves by your example. The highest respect for your opinion will be generated by your character, and people will demand to pay you for your opinion. It's a totally different side of supply and demand, isn't it?"

Michael slowly paced across the stage to allow people in the audience to make their choices. There was a silence in the room that confirmed that the crowd hung on Michael's every word. However, something unexpected happened as he paced. In the seconds that passed, with each step he took, Michael reflected on his own learning curve regarding sales. An awareness arose in Michael and brought him to the realization that he had just peaked as an authority on sales.

Left foot forward, and Michael could recall a time when he was completely ignorant of the sales process; he was in a state of unconscious, nonawareness.

Right foot landed, and Michael remembered the phone call from an old school friend who invited him to come down for a chat. As they caught up on what they'd been up to for the last couple of years, the conversation that day would take Michael through some pretty tough emotions as he learned two new things: that his old high school colleague had slept with his fiancée. That fact was forgivable because the friend did have the courage to admit it to Michael's face as soon as he found out that she was engaged to him. That, coupled with the fact that he'd been away for some time (a year or three—and the expression then formed would stick with Michael for years to come) meant that he couldn't have known and the affair was in fact her doing.

Michael's anger must have been apparent as the apology continued, broken by the query, "Are you going to hit me?"

Michael thought through it, and a wall of red was all he could see at the time, yet somehow he mustered an adequate response. "No. You came to me. You couldn't have known. You were honest with me. You're a good friend. Thank you."

The second thing that Michael realized that day was that his old buddy—Shooter, as Michael liked to call him, because of his military background—had also mentioned that Michael would be well suited for sales. Shooter had traveled a lot and earned even more, lost it all and built it back up again. It was a way out of a community Michael desperately wanted to leave. They met again to discuss his tutoring, and Michael was now conscious of his nonawareness.

Right foot lifting, and Michael recalled the "learning by doing" process and all its adventures: the constant traveling, seminars, sales, telemarketing, sales management, marketing and graphic design, marketing management, management, presales and referral campaigns, reputation buildup leading to consulting, organization and founding of his business, mass consulting, and regional sales management. Michael was conscious of his awareness in the field of sales.

Left foot down and stop; face the crowd. Michael had been working for the last few years in a state of unconscious awareness. His worth had grown, not just as a sales trainer but as a person.

His next words were to close the seminar and begin the next phase of his personal journey. He looked forward to being a student again. A deep smile rose from within him as he looked at the hundreds of faces that looked back at him. "I leave you today with these thoughts to ponder, and I trust you will make the choice that is right for you. Thank you all so very much for coming. I welcome each and every one of you to e-mail me personally and let me know how successfully the information works for you. Thank you again, and good night."

There came the sound of silence throughout the Plaza's great hall. There was humbleness about the way Michael closed the seminar—no more ego, no improvisation, just Michael giving thanks. There was no room for anything more; he had given his everything into those hours he stood on stage, and there was no more but himself there under the spotlights.

His recording was complete as students closed and set aside notebooks, the purposes for which would vary around the room. And the lull went on like a calm before the storm …

There was a saying in the business that the longer the lull, the greater the roar. There was always that moment after listening to a speaker that one waited to hear someone else cheer before starting oneself. So people took their time putting away their paperwork, setting aside their iPads, and closing their briefcases to avoid being the first one to shout out.

"You're the man, Michael! All right! Yeah! You nailed it! Right on, my man! Woohoo!"

Steven. Who else but Steven? Fearless and free of worry about being embarrassed, he shouted out clearly and passed it on. Jin caught it and found himself shouting, "Way to go, Michael! Yes!" before even realizing the significance of his actions.

It may have only been seconds that had passed, but suddenly both Steven and Jin were in a position to make each one count. It was their opportunity to give thanks back, and there was no stopping them.

Their cheers were contagious as an applause built up that dwarfed that of the day before. It was a slow, lumbering cheer that rose with such a crescendo and filled the room.

Briefcases aside, attendees were able to stand and give ovation. The jubilation in Michael's face could not be denied; he was truly happy with the result.

And he played it.

Moving his arms in a gesture to stop, the crowd did so. Then he beckoned them for more, and the crowd obliged. He silenced them again, and then played the right side of the room against the left. For a finale? A wave of cheers from stage left to stage right, before waving his hand for all they had. Satisfied, he clenched his fists in victory and ran down into the crowd, shaking hands as he made his way through the center of the room toward the lobby, where he would be swamped for hours to come.

Steven and Jin made their way over to Michael to give him a warm hug and slap on the back for a job well done. Jin heard Michael over Steven's shoulder say that a magazine was there to interview him and was asking permission to publish photos. They laughed as Michael said, "Maybe just a photo or three … but only if they'll market my DVD of this seminar for free!" Michael turned to Jin and said to him, "Thank you so much for coming, my friend. It's good having you here."

Michael briefly spoke to them aside, because it was all he had time for at the moment. "I'm so glad you guys could make it. The *Horn Verlag* is the largest, most reputable, and respected magazine in Germany. They might not have come if it wasn't for the fact that I had people coming from all over the world!" Michael's joy was abundant as he continued. "A car will pick you up in two hours at the main door here. Be in it. I'll meet you there in the restaurant next to the Turm."

At the heart of Cologne's Media Park was a tower with a section on the forty-second floor that could be used for events. The Turm, as it is known, may not beat the grandeur and height of Seattle's Space Needle, but the concept was the same. Cologne's very own Golden Boys, or die Goldene Jungs, were throwing a party that evening.

After a quick freshening up and a change of clothes, Jin and Steven were on their way. They were about to learn what the Golden Boys were about, and they were dressed for the occasion. At one of Cologne's finest restaurants, Michael had reserved a table. Steven and Jin were to take the underground metro service so as to see a different side of Cologne, and boy, would they ever!

Cologne's underground differed from other cities' undergrounds in that it was old, rattling along the tracks, and was not so much an underground as a metro service dropping down below one building, turning corners in the dark, and then popping up in a station just far enough away from where passengers started from so as to efficiently disorient them.

Within the city limits, one could walk to any location in about the same time it took to get there with the metro, but one would miss the night life and the city's favorite amateur sport: train hopping. Train security was so weak that only one city line could be controlled at a time, and the ticket checks were scheduled for weeks at a time. So if the line one was on was not the one being checked that week, there was little or no chance of being caught for not having a ticket. In other words, everyone rode the metro for free as much as they could.

Jin and Steven were no exceptions. Truth be told, it was difficult to even find a ticketing machine unless one really wanted to, and in the same amount of time it would take to find one, two trains would have come and gone.

At various stations, most people would drink; many people were drunk, but none of them were disorderly. There were no laws against drinking in public in Germany, only for being inordinate. People could have as much fun as they liked, and as long as they were respectful to others, they were welcome to roam wherever.

Out and about, women could be seen drinking beer like the guys, straight from the bottle. At first it seemed butch to a foreigner, but it was more likely a humble reminder that even the simplest of beers were prepared with German care and refined to levels of quality that were anti-culturally comparable to those found in fine French wines.

Everyone around was in such good spirits, with or without alcohol, and no policemen could be seen. Acceptance and tolerance were the staples of the evening. The stereotypical square-head image of a German citizen rapidly faded away. Everywhere Steven and Jin went, people were just people, doing the best they could with the tools they had.

Songs were sung on the train by old and young alike. It could have been a soccer team's anthem or an old folk song, for all Jin knew. It made no difference, because clearly not everyone on board knew the words. Those who didn't smiled and laughed with the rest as the song fell apart when the ensemble collectively lost the next verse's lyrics.

Steven and Jin arrived at Media Park. The lights in the lake and the modern buildings reflected an elegance that understated this was the place to be.

Somehow, Michael had arrived at the restaurant prior to Steven and Jin's arrival. By the time they arrived, Michael was found refreshed, changed, and already chatting up a young woman at the bar. Some heartfelt congratulatory embraces later, the men were seated.

Over dinner, they were joined by a couple of the girls from the sales team at the club who had had exceptional figures that month. According to Steven, their sales were probably pretty good as well. With one a beautician and the other a membership assistant at the club (which was which, only Michael knew), these girls were dressed to kill. Admittedly, the two girls were eye candy to be brought to the party. Both Sina and Anja were introduced politely, stating that they were big fans of the celebrity (whom Jin had never heard of) who would be at the party. The two of them then pretty much kept to themselves because it was immensely easier for them to speak in German than it was to carry on in English. Michael would occasionally interject in their conversation but for the most part, they took little interest in the three men's discussions.

The topic of the evening was young money. That's what the Jungs were about, and the only way to get into their sorority was by invitation or because daddy had loads of "cola" (cash). Parents could buy their kids' way into the club, as well as out of any trouble their golden child might get in while out with the rest of the boys.

Dinner was lovingly crafted by an Argentinean chef, who knew food as Jin had not yet experienced. Even the simplest of dishes at their table, a four-cheese pasta verdi, was made into a piece of art. Tastes were full, balanced, and refreshing, and the portions were arranged on the oversized plates to be visually appealing and light on the stomach.

Michael prepped them for the evening by reiterating as clearly as possible, "This is the biggest event to happen in Cologne this year. The papers will be there, and one or two TV stations for parts of it. We can safely say that it's the biggest party in Cologne. It's the best party to be at this evening in all of Germany. Security is at level two due to the star status of a couple of VIPs. The main thing is to have as much fun as possible—and I mean as much as possible … without getting arrested." His smile had the girls nearly blushing.

The bill was paid, and Michael led them to the lift that would bring them to the party. Entrance cards were given to a maître 'd at the top of some stairs. Two security guards patted each of them down before the doors on the lift swished open to allow them inside.

Steven and Michael purposefully started chuckling, and it hyped the five of them up as the lift carried them higher and higher.

"This is going to be so much fun!" Jin stated before the laughter won him over.

"The bomb, my man!" Steven agreed.

"Der hammer!" stated the girls in unison. Jin shrugged his shoulders, understanding the gist of what they must have meant, although the words were foreign to him.

Silence crept in as the ding on the lift sounded. The doors swished open to reveal a round room of luxury with panorama windows that overlooked the city lights as well as Media Park. Everyone was dressed decadently, was smiling, and was either in conversation with another or listening as live music played. Serving patrons rushed to make sure everyone had something to drink. Behind the band, a giant plasma screen silently played a promotional video of Til Schweiger's upcoming film release.

"Top of the world, gentlemen. Let's do this!" Michael's showmanship lit up whichever part of the room he was in, which made him easy to find. He performed a whimsical running commentary as he floated from one part of the room to another. He never sought to hold the limelight for himself for very long, if at all. He would constantly pass the center of attention on to others in the room: the amazing voice of the singer, who had come all the way from Jamaica (and was dating the party organizer, whom Jin had innocently enough spotted Michael speaking with in the lobby earlier); the gorgeous celebrity's wife, who was releasing a new line of Birkenstock shoes; the shoes themselves; her celebrity action-hero actor husband; his celebrity, manly-man, ex-athlete friend; as well as the posing hooker standing between the two men who hadn't noticed one of her newly purchased boobs poking out of the dress she must have bought before her augmentation.

Cologne's Golden Boys never compared wealth with one another. If one was present, it was enough. However, there did seem something of a game having to do with how much one could spend. The rules were simple: the person who spent the most money that evening, won. Nobody actually knew how much others had spent, so the game went on to simply buy everything one could in the room.

Michael's wealth perhaps lay more in his character than in his pocketbook. His personality was warmly welcomed by everyone; there was no conceit to be found.

Still, Jin could see the techniques for working a room that Steven had taught him before. Orphans, twos, groups of threes, and fours and more were forming and falling apart all the time. As introductions wafted around the room, it was difficult to know how much of it was just for show—making contacts, getting prospects.

Conversations led Jin to the conclusion that the Golden Boys weren't an egotistical bunch at all. Membership meant an illusionary protection and security from the sights and smells of poverty. Parents of the haves didn't mean for their children to hang out with the have-nots. The Goldene Jungs could do what they wanted out of sight from paparazzi photographers, and they'd control the media releases.

As much as Michael was on show for the evening,, his demeanor toward Steven and Jin showed his mind occasionally to be elsewhere. When questioned where his head was at, he replied that his mind was off someplace else, "Perhaps gone for a walk with my conscience." Michael regretted not being able to say more about it to his friends other than he hadn't figured it out for himself and would let them know as soon as he did. "It's an exciting time, though, isn't it? So come on, let's enjoy the party for what it is!"

Behind the words, Michael's cognitive senses were working to view his life as it was with a clear conscience. The evening before had left an impression induced by the sisters' perception, or at least by their thoughts about him. Michael had this immediate conceptualization as he sensed their first impressions of him that he wasn't sure of. The back of his mind raced to interpret and set in relation to other thoughts and experiences what to think beyond their original impressions.

Through the course of the evening, Michael's mind would arrange concepts, joining those concepts into constructs; by morning he would be weaving those constructs into complex, interpretative schemes. All this would be happening in Michael's head only half consciously during the conversations he led. As a result, Michael's subconscious took the time necessary to be sure his perception was clear without getting carried away.

All through the night, Michael would be actively observing and controlling where his thoughts went. He thought about his physical health and balanced that with how he felt about himself. He thought about both his state of mind and the various phenomena about him. Tonight, in Germany, this was without a doubt the place to be.

Tonight, Michael asked himself, *Is it where I want to be?*

The wake-up call came through at seven o'clock. It was Michael on the line, bright and cheerful as though he hadn't missed a beat. He invited Steven and Jin to meet him. "Come by work, and we'll go for brunch at nine. I'll arrange a taxi to take you to the airport when it's time for your departure."

While Steven readied himself in the washroom, Jin felt the strain of the near-sleepless nights. He felt it in his abs, and he felt it more in his arms. He was deeply conscious of every push-up and he felt the muscles tightening above his elbows as the tendons had to pick up where the muscles left off. A hot shower would ease but not remove the effects of the extra effort required this morning.

The two of them arrived to find Michael still seemingly unaffected by the length of the weekend's activity. *How does he do it?* Jin thought. Steven asked Michael that same question at breakfast.

"I use good creams—no, I use great skin creams that keep me looking fresh even when I am not. But I didn't invite the two of you here this morning to talk about the all-natural ingredient advantages of Decléor products for men.

"It's the weirdest thing, Steven. I took this job on originally in order to give my marriage a chance to right itself, while at the same time ensuring I had a future career if it didn't. I'd put so much effort into that relationship and wasn't getting a return emotionally or physically. My marriage failed via text message one week later, and I was lucky enough to get an annulment to avoid what could have been a tedious process here in Germany.

"You see, Jin, we had eloped; there wasn't any paperwork to confirm we were married. I don't doubt that she loved me, just as I know I loved her; part of me still does. Some people just don't fit together, y'know?"

"Square peg in round hole?" Jin prompted.

"More like round peg in no hole." Michael continued after a short pause for dramatic effect. "And that for a year. My point is, you can never force anyone against her will. Never. I'm eternally grateful to my ex for teaching me that. Employees are no different; after all, they're people too. If they can't be bothered, then get rid of them. The sooner the better, if you ask me. They'll only damage the reputation of whatever business you're in, and you'll end up having to repair more things later the longer you keep them on staff.

"Anyway, I've fired more often than I've hired, and here I am, top of my game—regional sales manager." He said it with an illusionary regal tone. "My teammates on my level love my enthusiasm and can't get over how gung ho I am. I've become one of the most respected sales managers in Europe. I live in the heart of Cologne in a penthouse suite, for goodness sake! I'm earning enough to live a lifestyle most would dream of, and I support my girlfriends."

"Excuse me? Girlfriends?" Jin picked up on the plural.

"Yeah, I know. It's a terrible life but someone has to live it, right?" Michael shook his head to indicate he didn't mean what he was saying, at least anymore. "My motto has become 'Live a little, love a lot.' That's parallel to everyone's carpe diem. I think it's been a reaction to breaking up with someone who wouldn't sleep with me for such a long period of time. There's this sexy club manager up north who comes down to attend my seminars; there are the wannabe posh girls in the beauty salon, which wasn't exactly my fault because I only meant to date one of them until the second one took over a massage appointment the first one got called away from. Oh, and last but not least, there's the cutest lil' girl of my sales team; my operations manager would kill to be with her as well. Truth be known, the girls I actually love to bits are the lesbian couple I'm the closest of friends with, and would gladly have babies with! The other ones are just along for the ride; they get theirs, and I get mine.

"I'm in with all the right crowds and have become this macho male hero to many of them. I live by a golden rule that I will never cross my friends, and they know it, so most guys want to be my friend. I tell ya, the Persian people know how to host!"

The two of them smiled at their recollection of understanding the meaning of the word "pasha" in its essence. Michael said, "You may recall, the other night, I brought home those two sisters. Well ... Melek, Selima, and I had this profound conversation that had me looking pretty critically at myself—and yes, Steven, we only *talked* the entire evening. It was the most amazing thing; I hadn't talked to a girl in forever! It helped me answer a lot of things I've been questioning in my person. The thing is, I'd been asking myself lately what I've actually done. I've taught a couple of hundred people how to ask, 'This one or this one?' But what have I contributed? Better yet, what am I contributing to the world right now? How can I at least be doing this better?

"Regarding my work, I've already thought of and addressed this. If we know that objections will come down to one of five reasons, why aren't we doing something about that? That's essentially what day one of my seminar is about: it's something that's so important to me, to help others do their jobs better, more effectively, and more affluently so that they enjoy a higher standard of life.

Why don't we simply ask questions earlier on, as we're building rapport? That would discourage any objection coming up in the first place. My team does. We preclose as much as possible during the time we are getting to know the person. Keep in mind we don't sell aircraft engines or houses, but the same principles could be applied to those industries; you would simply be dealing with a company, rather than an individual.

"The trouble is that whenever salespeople do better, companies just raise the bar over and over, until it drains people of their humanity. The high pressure of targets sterilizes the process, makes it mechanical. People recognize when it's fake. It's become the job of management to keep it real, and that has become the greatest challenge. We can easily ask a person how long a person has been thinking about this. No matter people's answer is, we can suggest to them that the moment right now is obviously a great one to make a decision. Or we simply ask them, if they've had enough time thinking about it, to make a decision today. Whatever works for you. If there's no genuineness about it, forget it.

"We may not be able to ask them if they have enough money, although in certain circumstances a budget should be known, but at least knowing if they'd like to meet before or after work will generally let us know that they are working. The person who receives the prospect's first inquiry can ask this easily enough when booking the appointment. If you're not taking appointments, you might consider usage as an option. When might they be using the service you're offering? Otherwise it's possible to ask how much they were budgeting for their decision, just to know whether or not they're in the ballpark. But if they sense it's all about the money, you'll strike out.

"Time is often a factor in most businesses, as it is with ours, so we ask how often they would like to use the service because it may affect the best possible package that we can offer them, and we want to be sure to present them the best possibility. For purchasers, this will have an effect on possible insurances and warranties offered. But if we pressure the prospect, they'll feel backed into a corner and lash back, most likely with an ill word to say about not you but the business.

"Commitment is the other time factor, so work to raise their commitment by listening to the whys over and over again. This is a great moment to build on their personal justification of their decision, and it's done easily enough, but if you're not actively listening, if they don't feel understood, they'll walk away.

"Lastly, there are those people who need to check it out or run it by their partner. I admit we are pretty aggressive on this point and will often ask on the phone if the decision is theirs or not, and if it isn't we suggest they invite them down. If their partner can't make it (and surprisingly, their partner never does), then the prospect should call the prosepect's partner/significant other. Everyone these days has a mobile phone. It's less aggressive to simply ask how their partner feels about this decision. This technique works well with businesses as well. What does their business feel about working together with yours? What has the prospect heard about you and your business; what's the word on the street? These questions show that you genuinely care about your good name and the reputation of your business. It makes you more human, and you can build rapport on this. By doing this as much as possible up front, we save ourselves some possible aggravation later, and we save the prospect their time as well—for the time being. Perhaps, when their situation changes, it might be a better time to come back; who knows?

"I've been cultivating a team of genuine people; they stay focused on their sincerity meter, on nurturing it and checking it constantly. Some sales take longer than others; that's the way it is. I don't criticize, I emphasize. That's the direction I've been going, and I believe that's why our results are so phenomenal. Well, that and because I work with a team of really sexy girls!"

Laughter at the absurdity permitted all three of them to be reminded that although the team was great looking, it was the sincerity that sold them, every time.

"Seeing you again, Steven—and meeting you, Jin—has really done me a load of good. It's made me really trust in what I'm doing many times over. It's given me the extra courage I needed to add the preclosing part in my seminar. It's not normally part of it; I just allow for more question periods after the other two bits, and I've reached the conclusion that this"—he waved his arms about, indicating everything around him—"all of this is not me. This is not who I am.

"I've always been an extremist; Steven, you know that about me already. It's why I'm so extreme gung ho and when I look at my lifestyle right now, I realize I'm at one side of the pendulum's sweep. If I'm to come back to being me, I've got to bring it back as extremely as possible. So I've decided to quit my job. I'm going to simplify my life and live chaste for one year."

Steven and Jin both sat stunned; they had not seen it coming. Michael seemed so well suited for his lifestyle.

Michael noticed their looks and said, "Go on, tell me. You think I'm crazy, right? I mean to give myself a year to meet someone who actually likes me for who I am, and then take time to get to know her. Oh, and she can never know about my vow until after the fact. Hopefully she will have the respect for me by then to be understanding. It seems like a good investment, if you ask me.

"Maybe I'll write a book or something. I'll call it *The Book on Sales*, and then I could sing along with friends, 'Well, I wonder, wonder who? Who wrote the book on sales?' and it would be none other than yours truly. Or else I could go around saying, 'What are you talking about? I wrote the book on sales, buddy!'"

Smiles went around the table as the trio silently acknowledged that it had been a fantastic whirlwind tour d'Allemagne.

Steven finally said, "Whatever makes you happy, my man." There was a lean-over and embrace with some more slapping on the back. "You know I love ya like a brother. I wouldn't want to be you right now, but I'm here for you if you need me."

An announcement for a taxi came to their table, and the group gave each other genuine embraces. With that, they were on their way back to Seattle.

Steven was already in slumber mode in the taxi, and Jin was able to sleep in spurts during the flight. His fear of flying was subdued by exhausted dreams of being comforted again by his mom, who assured him everything was just as it was meant to be.

Jin dreamt of a sales environment that had no distinction between one department and another. In his mind's eye, he could see it working more effectively than anything he had seen at the NSC. He just needed to concentrate on the right elements, and the system would work. He brought himself to a single-minded state where his mental faculties remained unified. He then directed those mental faculties toward increasing the success of the center. The success of the center was inevitably directly his own.

Jin meditated on the subject further as Steven continued to slumber peacefully. He focused, directed his thoughts, and sustained his concentration. Jin intensified his concentration step by step when an unexpected, everyday situational thought crossed his mind.

He wondered what Steffi was up to, almost casually at first. It was curious that her image would pop into his head so innocently. A quick review of the beautiful girls he had met, and the semicelebrity parties, oddly enough helped him realize that he wasn't interested in any of them. He missed Steffi.

Jin put into perspective the experiences he had made as a salesperson and reflected on his life experiences to figure out what made a good salesperson. Jin drew parallels through his life and his limited knowledge of the lives of others, gaining insight and wisdom as he did so.

Jin's family was Buddhist. Considering themselves good Buddhists, Jin saw many similarities between the core beliefs of his family and those of Fahid Amil's family back in Seattle, who prided themselves on being good Sikhs; Mr. Brown, who prided himself on being a good Christian; and the sisters, who took pride in their Muslim heritage. Religion, race, and creed had nothing to do with being a great salesperson.

Jin examined those around him to ask what made those he admired so great. What made Gran so great at being a great grandmother? What made Uncle D great at what he did? What was it about Jin's mother that made her a fantastic mom? What made Sensei Iura a great martial artist?

It all came down to the same thing: "Greatness, whose potential is within all of us, lays in the character of the individual, not in the task they perform." Being a black belt at anything meant sharing the knowledge gained with as many people as possible, being open to any comment or criticism, and allowing for the consideration of another person's opinion. It was about learning about any given subject as an ongoing process.

Jin had chosen to live sales as Michael had suggested—to become a samurai at the career he had begun. Change was in the air.

Little could prepare the two men for the center back home. Steven had been silent beyond being just being tired; he had been considering Michael's words, looking deeply at his own career, and making some private decisions related to those thoughts.

Even in a slumbered state, change didn't necessarily require focus. Both men were literally flying straight into change blindly. Their first test was just sixteen hundred miles away. Radical change could occur whether one focused on any given subject or not.

It was how one reacted to change that defined one's character for what it was.

Perseverance
Red Belt

The Five Forms of Attack

- SAA, or singular angle attack.
- PIA, or progressive indirect attack.
- HIA, or hand immobilization attack.
- ABC, or attack by combination.
- ABD, or attack by drawing.

A change of management—it happens.

A Southerner had taken over the management of the NSC. Mr. Bob Jenkins was part owner and was now protecting his assets. Mr. Brown unfortunately had some health problems that would keep him away, possibly indefinitely.

Mr. Jenkins came from a part of the States commonly known as the Old South, where things moved at a slower pace than most; specifically, he was from Alabama. People didn't walk down the boulevards of Mr. Jenkins's small home town—they sauntered. Even dogs moved slower, if they moved at all, to get out of the afternoon sun.

Southerners may move a little slower, but it shouldn't be confused with laziness or inefficiency. They referred to this phenomenon as conservation of energy. Southerners' ability to make a decision and follow it through was one of their strengths. Such was the case with following through and taking over the management upon Mr. Brown's falling ill.

Mr. Jenkins's character came à la carte with Southern drawl. He was a large man who enjoyed the finer things in life, including fine whiskey and sometimes legally imported cigars.

It was an opportunity for Jin to bring to the table the vision he had during the return flight. When he met with Steven and Mr. Jenkins, Jin gave his pitch. "I propose we remove all the barriers in the NSC that prevent salespeople—real salespeople—from selling. I believe that a true salesperson can and will sell more if the opportunity is there. I am confident that I could outsell any department hands down, if I were permitted to sell in every department. I'd stake my job on it. What have you got to lose? If I fail, you're out a rookie amateur whom you may not need anyway. If I succeed, you earn more money from me. There are others here who could do just the same if allowed to. Let me prove it to you. If I'm wrong, fire me."

Steven raised an eyebrow at Jin's confidence. He'd seen Jin grow in so many ways since the boy had started his employment at the NSC. Jin had learned to express his personality in a positive way that influenced others to trust in his confidence. Steven was glad Jin was on his side.

"Y'all sure 'bout this boy, Mr. Page?" asked Mr. Jenkins.

Jin could feel the nod from Steven, even though Steven sat behind him. Jin smiled at the gained confidence, knowing he had Steven Page's support.

Mr. Jenkins chewed on one of his newly imported cigars. He looped the cigar round from one corner of his mouth to another and then paused as if to check that the end of the cigar was indeed moist enough. Then he opened his drawer for a long-stick cedar match.

He struck the match somewhere out of sight from Jin and Steven. The stillness in the room allowed Jin and Steven to hear the flames eagerly consume the end of the matchstick. As the two of them looked on, the remainder of the sulfur from the match was nearly used up before Mr. Jenkins placed the flame near enough to the end of his Robusta to light it. Things move slower in the South. And with a few puffs, Mr. Jenkins put the ball in motion. "I like the cut o' your jib, son. Y'all got a week. I'll give y'all a chance at yer theory. Prove to me it works, an' good luck. Page, y'all sort out the details, an I'll see y'all next week."

A week? Steven thought. *Sink or swim, we're in.*

There was no reason to hold back their attacking the challenge. Success would require the utilization of all the sales techniques Jin had learned. Some challenges could be faced directly, but others would need to be addressed less directly. Steven would do his best to immobilize the "raising of the hand" of any of the resistant managers so that Jin could focus on selling by drawing on his abilities.

Before the battle, Jin meant to have a heart-to-heart with his cousin.

Like any would-be brothers, Art and Jin had their differences. Jin was always the cousin favored for doing well in school, whereas Art was never pressured to do better than he did. Jin, being slightly older, had carved the way for Art, and Art was the child most likely to stretch those boundaries. If Jin had stayed up until eight at the age of ten, then Art stayed up until eight at the age of nine.

To some, it may have seemed Jin was the more intelligent of the two boys. To Jin, Art was always the one with the better head on his shoulders. Jin could never remember actually telling Art how much he respected that about him. Jin always felt the pressure of his good grades because to others they were no big deal for him—he should be doing better still. A feeling of inadequacy built up inside him so that he never felt he could do well enough and be enough for anyone. He'd left home at an early age to discover the world, and he learned to always expect more of himself than anyone else could … and he did.

Where Jin was more the aloof character, Art was more responsible. Both boys were loved equally by their parents, as well as their respective aunt and uncle. Gran's love for the boys never faltered, and she never judged either one of them.

Jin had a difficult time understanding the life that Art had chosen for himself; knuckling down in one place and being content to stay there, while Jin desired nothing less than seeing the world. Art's life was nothing for Jin.

Likewise, Art couldn't understand how Jin could be so irresponsible in his actions, considering Art had worked so hard to create security around himself and all he did. He had worked many years building relationships with local companies that knew they could depend on him for their needs and a job to be done. To Art, Jin's life was nothing for him.

It wasn't that they didn't love each other, because at their cores, they really did. They simply had difficulties expressing those feelings toward one another.

Gran had once said to Jin how she admired Jin's gypsy heart. She liked that he could just pick up and go with nothing more than a backpack to wherever his desires led him. Jin now desired to speak with Art as family; they were family, after all, like it or lump it.

Art worked long hours as well as many days. Jin decided to wait on him at his uncle's until Art arrived home. Art arrived home late in the evening. Uncle D was out at some business dinner that was sure to go on until sometime in the morning. It was a great opportunity for the boys to sit down together and talk.

Jin told Art how he had seen much in the world and regretted none of it. He wouldn't trade any of his experiences for the security art had created for himself, but at the same time he admired how Art, with all the temptations in the world to go out there and see it, was disciplined not to do so.

It took Art aback to hear Jin speak this way. They were never affectionate toward one another, either physically or verbally.

Jin went on to describe things in the world that he had experienced in his travels, and how everywhere he'd been, there were certain constants. Everywhere Jin went, there were families. Each family may be different, but all shared a particular thing in common.

"And what's that, Jin?" Art asked.

"They relate to one another. For good or worse, in sickness or in health; they relate to one another."

A stillness passed before Art responded, "That's probably where the word 'relations' comes from."

"You're probably right." Jin went on to talk to Art about the challenge before him, and he asked Art's thoughts on the matter. Art conceded that sales weren't his field of expertise, and he wasn't sure he was the right person to ask. Jin explained how he felt that actually Art *was* an expert. He was just doing naturally what others formally trained to do.

Their conversation went into the commonality of all people, how people were programmed to respond to one thing, the question. It didn't matter whether one was Japanese, American, German, Turkish, or a Japanese American dating a Turkish girl who spoke German. People all responded to the question.

Jin said, "From the time we are born and begin to cry, there has universally been someone there to ask us, 'What's the matter? Are you hungry? Do you need changing?' No human being has been hatched from an egg, and so we are all programmed to answer questions. Answering questions is a defense mechanism for our very survival. We are all dependent on being able to answer questions. Success in any form is simply a matter of asking the right questions the right way with the right intention, and taking right action as to the responses."

Art could see how his building relationships over the years were based on how much he knew about his contacts, and that getting to know them, the discovery of who they were and what they were about, was based on his asking questions; it was impossible to get to know someone otherwise.

Art said, "When you came here to Seattle to live with us, I never thought it would last. I thought it would just be a passing thing for you, and you would take off at the first opportunity. But you haven't; you've stayed and proven yourself. I can now see how it has only been circumstances that caused you to go on your journey. Ultimately that journey has been about discovering yourself, and I believe you have. What's more, I like the man you have become, and I love you as family. Ask questions, Jin, and you will succeed at your plan. I know you will. You've always had a knack for figuring these kinds of things out. It's something I've hated yet admired about you all my life."

Uncle D came in the door, stating that it was time for everyone to get some sleep. The boys wished each other a good night. A moment of awkward silence passed between them as they stood up to make their way. Uncle D smiled as he observed the boys give each other a quick pat-on-the-back hug before retiring to whatever the morning would bring.

The next day, Steven communicated the tactics throughout the NSC as best as possible with the limited time allotted. Jin would be permitted to sell any product in any department in the NSC during the week. At the end of the week, each department's best day of net sales would be compared to Jin's, for which a precedent would possibly be set.

Steven said, "I know you can do it, my man. Now, go for it! Oh, and another thing before you do: I mean to quit after you do, my man. So see to it that you're in a position to take over my job after you do, okay?"

Jin now saw how Steven had taken Jin under his wing as his protégé, nurturing him for the purpose of taking over his function at the NSC. There were, in Steven's eyes, no other department heads qualified to lead the others, and a new senior advisor would have to come from a different source.

Jin thought carefully on the task before him. This was undoubtedly an opportunity for him to perform as the modern-day warrior—a black-belt salesperson. Like a samurai, he would have to cut through the various departments and attack the situation at its heart: sales.

Jin was fearful of failing, missing some crucial point, and blowing it. He wanted to succeed more than anything. Speaking to his uncle on the matter gave Jin added comfort in knowing he was not alone, as he listened to Uncle D's words. "Not to worry, son. For all great people, the past haunts, the present frightens, and the future seeks to confuse. It is when you stand up despite these things that you will succeed."

Samurai Sales

Rise of the Modern-Day Warrior

The Northgate Shopping Center had departments for nearly everything. If they'd had room to stock Boeing jet engines, they would do it. In its diversity, the center had become disconnected. Jin's concept was simple: break down the barriers and allow salespeople to sell and to connect, discover, and respond to customer needs, whatever they may be across any department. Working together as one giant team, the NSC could accomplish more. As the acronym for TEAM went, "Together, Everyone Accomplishing More!"

Steven had mentioned he'd be in meetings with department heads throughout the week, as well as getting to know the new NSC head. Any extra time he'd have would most likely be taken up entertaining Mr. Jenkins, which meant he wouldn't have time to back Jin's plan up except from behind the scenes.

The warm greetings from the hygienic engineering team encouraged Jin to press on; it was great to see Rashid again. Anxious and proud of his team's developments, Fahid made a point that Jin know that they were all behind him, and if there was anything they could do to help, Jin need only ask.

Jin was eager to see one other particular member of the NSC team. Steffi was equally happy to see Jin again and embraced him warmly. She welcomed the wholeheartedness of Jin's newly acquired

European embrace, the genuine warmth of which reminded Steffi of the comfort of her childhood experienced just outside of Wießen. She flushed at Jin's discovered confidence and agreed to go for dinner, where they could talk more.

The two of them had dinner, and Jin could finally explain to her his plans for the breakdown of the current system so that there would be no more walls at Alsportraz. Steffi commented that since Matt had been out on the floor and actually working again, the atmosphere had improved immensely.

The next week would tell all. The pressure for Jin to prove his theory in front of his peers was on. His personal sales abilities secured, Jin felt confident in his theory that a salesperson shouldn't be restricted in what he or she sells in an organization.

At one end of the scale, it was easy to see how McDonald's employees didn't need to have a second person to come over to ask, "You want fries with that?" At the other end of the scale, it was understandable that something as specialized as, say, spacecraft engines required some expertise. The purchaser in any larger organization, however, would never be the one to require that expert breakdown. Sales remained an emotional process justified by logic, even at the highest level of transaction. Everybody sold.

A salesperson was employed to do just that. Their ability to do so was only limited by their personality and the availability of products in front of them. Why should something get in their way?

Jin's colleagues were not so sure of these new changes and opted for the security of what was familiar to them. He couldn't really blame them for the resistance; the only people who liked changes were wet babies. The rest of the team went about their business pretty much the same way as they always had. Some even schemed to work against the possibility that the current system might eventually change. These department managers kept their teams to themselves and thought to prove Jin's theory wrong by gunning for a great sales day. They pushed their teams to sell as much as they could, service be damned! They wanted numbers, and big ones!

As Jin went about his business, he was profoundly aware of the turning of the wheel at each stage of the sales process. Jin worked the center as a single room, prospecting for leads that, through super-qualification would lead to introducing himself and creating that crucial first impression.

After learning the prospect's interests, Jin was able to quickly place him or her as either qualified or not. Digging deeper and deeper, Jin connected, discovered, and responded over and over again. He could be seen from time to time throughout the entire center, chatting away with a gentleman as they walked. Jin would casually appear, ask something of the sales representative in the department about a product or two, and then continue on to another department. He was preclosing, handling objections, closing, and referring along the way.

Throughout the week, many departments had performed well on one day or another. Some had even landed some fantastic sales figures on a day. The extra push had many a department manager returning proudly to the end-of-week sales meeting. The relentless driving, however, would result in numerous staff calling in ill the next week for one reason or another. Stress was the number-one killer, with illness being the first signs of it. Pressure combined with poor diet was a cocktail for disastrous turnovers that Steven and Mr. Jenkins agreed the NSC had best not drink, for risk of the hangover that might ensue.

Seven days passed. The trial came to an end, and Steven, ever supportive of Jin's idea, discovered he was first in the board room, waiting patiently for the others arrival. A part of Steven waited much like a nervous parent-to-be, but he was there for Jin. It remained to be seen what had spawned from their efforts.

One by one the heads came in from departments as abstract as some of their titles. Steven decided it best to wait for Jin and confer with him as privately and discreetly as possible upon his arrival.

Mr. Jenkins gave a brief greeting to the group, casually clipped a cigar, sat comfortably, and requested the net sales results of each department's best day from those who had already arrived. The game was afoot. Papers shuffled forward with numbers called across the table from those departments particularly proud of the resulting figures of their best sales day. Other figures were better described as average. After all, the Northgate Shopping Center was large enough to satisfy the desires of each of the average person's shopping wishes, no matter what that might be, so there were bound to be ups or downs. The meeting today wasn't about the exact statistics, but judging tendencies and an aptitude for change.

Anal lists, Steven mused to himself.

The center was large enough that it took a significant amount of time for heads of departments to gather for meetings; that was one of the reasons they only held meetings once a week. Today was that day. The managers of each department gathered to discuss their results. Many previous meetings were about patting each other on the back for a job well done. In the conference room they continued to arrive one after another. Many had shown up out of curiosity, and others were there to prove the new ideology wrong. One of them would even scoff at the bourgeois manner of conducting sales within such a reputable establishment as the NSC.

The meeting was about money. The objective was to use the results to examine the possibility of an area for capital growth. There would be no patting on the back today unless Mr. Jenkins saw fit to do the patting. And as Mr. Jenkins saw it, "I ain't kin to no one here. Y'all jus' ante up and show me the money!" Facts and figures—that's all Mr. Jenkins wanted to hear.

Numerous people spoke in low tones. Some department heads brought out any possibly required proof of receipts to back their claims. Home appliance figures were first to rise above the commotion. Mr. Kaere's department had experienced generally strong sales days. The best day was when they sold several sets of appliances to new homeowners (albeit at a discounted rate), as well as numerous single appliances; a respectable eighteen thousand dollars was generated from 137 sales.

One Mr. Bourignon boasted of his young girlfriend's ability to consistently maintain sales at a rate above his predecessor's. With a forced "new collection" launch during the week, it was rather unsurprising that the lingerie team had a record-best result at twelve thousand dollars and well over two hundred sales. Unbeknownst to Mr. Bourignon was that two and a half thousand dollars of that grand total had been charged to his own credit card for the entire new season collection. Further unknown was that his girlfriend had already modeled some of the apparel for Mr. Kaere ...

One by one departments reported quality figures: furnishings, home depot, and numerous clothing stores. Real estate had generated more leads, but only one deposit on some property had been transacted; nonetheless it was a good day with two sales going through. Many department figures were above ten thousand dollars, with a few above twenty thousand.

Jin arrived in time to hear that his old colleague, Jim-Bob at the rod and gun sports shop, had broken his personal sales record, selling sets of book-matched rifles to a collector who had been visiting the shop for weeks. The collector's set alone made up eighteen thousand dollars of the department's twenty-six thousand dollars in sales that day.

Then Mr. Yves Scheers spoke. He rose to introduce himself as the head of the luxury automobile department. Yves's designer shirt, much like his ego, was overstuffed while his hair was kept much alike his attention span toward other people— immeasurably short. His department consistently had the top results whenever there were any such occurrences at the NSC. With thirteen sales, the luxury auto department triumphantly landed a record sales day of fifty-eight thousand dollars that was sure to put all of this silliness to one side, once and for all.

As the noise at the table died down, eyes turned to Steven and Jin, who were found quietly conversing with one another all the while.

"And what about you, son?" Mr. Jenkins said as he faced Jin. "What do y'all got for me?"

Jin glanced toward Steven for permission and then slowly stood from his table and waited for silence. He wanted everyone's absolute attention before he spoke. "One sale."

Mr. Jenkins practically spat in response. "What? Y'all got what? God dang, kid! What y'all been doin'? I mean, jeez, boy. One? *One sale?*"

Steven silently observed the smirks that ran across the table. It was apparent which department heads had been rooting against Jin's concept. He made a mental note of the faces involved before relaxing back in his chair. Mr. Jenkins's attention swayed in his direction. "I trusted you, Page! What the heck y'all playin' at?"

Steven shrugged the comment off and redirected Mr. Jenkins's attention to Jin before lowering his head and await Jin's comeback. He was still confident in his protégé's actions.

Jin returned Mr. Jenkins's glare with a patient silence. Mr. Jenkins then calmed down enough to say, "Well, I'm almost 'fraid to ask, but how much did y'all get from that one sale?"

Yves tilted back in his chair, placing his hands behind his head to focus on what was sure to be Jin's downfall.

Jin spoke without ego as he stated his day's net sales figure. "One hundred twenty-seven thousand, six hundred, and, uh, thirty-six dollars." He glanced down at his note book to be sure. "And sixty-seven cents."

Yves chair jerked out from beneath him. Mr. Jenkins's cigar fell from his lips, making no noise as it landed on the board-room floor. It was difficult to say which hit the floor first, Yves or the butt of Mr. Jenkins's Robusta.

The energy that rose from the board room exploded. Laughter at Yves's fall spilled over into congratulations from others, with shouts of doubt and requests of proof in between.

Steven slowly pushed all the receipts to the middle of the table to silence any doubt. Mr. Jenkins's voice shook with enthusiasm. "What? Ya sold how much? How in tarnation did y'all manage that?"

Jin passed by Mr. Scheers, picking up the pen that had fallen from his pocket, and he continued on to where Mr. Jenkins sat. He handed him back the Robusta before he spoke. "Well, I met this guy from the waterfront development projects and found out he needed a fishing hook. So I brought him down to our rod and gun place, where Jim-Bob was just in the process of unwrapping the new Bass Master 3500 series fishing rod. I asked my client how big a fish he'd like to catch, and he said about a thirty-five pounder, so Jim-Bob and I provided him with an assortment of appropriate hooks.

"Then I asked him about the test strength of the line he had at home, and he said he wasn't sure, so I said, well, he'd best be sure. Jim-Bob recommended some fifty-pound test line, which we sold him. Then Jim-Bob asked him about his fishing rod, and we found out his rod wasn't strong enough for the line, so we sold him that new Bass Master series reel and rod.

"Then I asked him where he was planning to go fishing. and he said he knew a quiet place up north he liked. I said he'd probably want some warmer clothing, so we checked out all the new thermals that had come in. He'd be there at the lake up north for a couple of days, so he'd probably want a change of clothing; I sold him one set of the new season's and one set of last season's gear. He was grateful for the discount on last season's gear, and he and I started talking about his boat, which he'd had for some time.

"As it turned out, it was rather exposed to the elements, especially if he planned to be out on the water for the weekend, so I brought him over to the boat shop. We looked at that new Bayliner in the display window from Correct Craft, and he fell in love with the freedom of being able to be on lake for the whole weekend—no phones, no hassles, just fishing. I could see he loved it, so I asked him if he wanted me to find out what deal I could get for him if he traded in his old boat. He said sure, so I worked out a deal with the boat department if he bought the display model right away. After that I asked him how he'd be bringing the boat to the lake, and he said he'd take it in tow, so I asked him what trailer he had. The one he owned definitely wasn't strong enough, so I went back in and renegotiated the deal with trailer and all the options and insurances, which he was really pleased to have.

"When the crew asked him about mounting the trailer hitch on his truck, he said, 'Truck? I ain't got no truck. I got a car.' So I brought him over to our auto department, where we've got that bright red Dodge 2500 series Ram truck. With a three-quarter-ton capacity, I said he could probably kit the whole thing out for some off-road fishing-hole possibilities, as well as some storage options for the newest in safety gear for the boat. He agreed to buy the full package if the auto department could have all the kits loaded and ready by closing time that day. The mechanic there—I think his name is

Lionel—said yes, so we went back to the rod and gun department to complete the order.

"He soon realized with the off-road possibilities now available to him, he'd be able to try fly fishing, which he'd always wanted to since he was a boy. So after selling him some more kits, including hip waders and a five-session package of private fly-fishing lessons from the athletics department, I was able to get his dream fishing experience together with some savings on the road.

"He paid for the whole thing up front with his platinum card—apparently he's one of the owners of the building company developing the harbor docks."

"You sold all that to a guy looking for a fishing hook?" an eager-to-learn Mr. Kaere demanded.

"No. He actually came in looking for some, uh, feminine products for his wife. I told him his weekend was fucked, and he'd be better off going fishing."

Looks of astonishment appeared across the table, and the people in the room were caught speechless. Steven was stifling some pretty proud laughter as Jin continued. "Oh, and his best friend is coming in tomorrow, and he'll be joining him when he goes. Apparently he likes sailing more than fishing. His friend has been looking to buy a little getaway on a lakefront somewhere, so I'm hoping the real estate department can help me out a bit tomorrow." Jin glanced at the real estate department's manager and received a blank nod before turning back to Mr. Jenkins. "Well, you didn't think I'd forget the referral, did you?"

All eyes were fixed on Jin, and he heard murmuring, but people had nothing to say. Steven crossed his arms and waited patiently for Mr. Jenkins to speak. *Jin, my man, you've done it. Well done!*

After patting him on the back, Mr. Jenkins spoke the only words of any particular relevance. "Jin, my son. Ya ever thought about management?"

The Creed
Black Belt

> "I dedicate myself to constant and never-ending improvement. I develop courage and master self-discipline. I pledge loyalty and support to family, friends, and my fellows. I will share what I have learned with others, lead by example, and become a role model in my community."
>
> —Jin

Reflecting on the oath of his martial arts studies helped Jin see that the oath applied to his profession as well—to anybody profession. To truly master something was, in part, to share that knowledge with as many people as possible. The question at hand was how to reach out to as many people as possible.

Hmm, thought Jin. *Management is one way to share knowledge with many more people than I could do in my current position. And I am confident I could master management given time. Management mastery—I like the sound of that. It's a great opportunity!* Jin would give the challenge due consideration … for about a second or three.

End

Appendix A

What You Already Knew

There is nothing new about the Eight Steps of Selling; the process has been around since the first sale was made. Ever since the first buying and selling relationship was established, the sales process has been refined and defined in many ways, including the sales wheel. The wheel, in my opinion, is one of the most interesting things invented; it needn't ever be reinvented.

Sales training and sales-training methods are as varied as the people who offer them. I've witnessed sales-training methods ranging from being taught by getting participants to sing and dance, to publicly humiliating and insulting paying participants. I'm not here to criticize others' methods. What works for one person most probably will not work for every person.

I would like to address the point that throughout most of the systems taught, there seems to be an agreement that the sales process is cyclic. So why eight steps—why not nine or ten? Why not thirty-four? Is it that the Buddhist "Noble Eightfold Path" to enlightenment has proven eight to be the most practical number of steps for learning?

Not likely. The answer may actually lay in sales psychology itself, in particular marketing and advertising psychology.

I have been told by institutes that ought to know about these things—including Oxford University School of Business Marketing, the Interior Architectural Design Campus at the University of Hamburg, and two graphic design professors from Yale University—that the human eye can pick up about eight images on any given surface. Any further images confuse the eye, and therefore none of the images are effectively picked up; the images become cluttered and thus ineffective. What's interesting is that the same rules apply for advertising as for interior decorum. Put more than eight details on a wall, and it will look cluttered.

I was fascinated by this, so I put it to the test and found the observations to be about right. After going through a newspaper casually and then sitting down afterward to record every advert I could remember, I was able to record the ads from which there were eight or less images on each page—no more than six, to be precise. I've become more conscious about the number of plants, paintings, and pictures that each wall in my home "advertises," which has in turn created a very comfortable living space. I'm certain it's all very feng shui, but that's not really my point. My point is that we are absolutely inundated with marketing these days. Whether my observations are more a sign of the times or a sign of my age, I'll leave it up to you, but here's a thought: If after taking the test yourself (and I invite you to do so), you don't see the little advert on the pages with thirty-three other advertisements, how is your potential consumer ever going to see it?

I invite you to think of this the next time a company invites your company to advertise with them. What results can an advertising agency guarantee, and would they work on a commission basis?

What You May Not Have Known

All characters in *Samurai Sales* are based on facets of people I have met as well as facets of myself. However, some have meanings with a bit more history, and I thought to share a bit with you here for an insider's view.

For the character Uncle D, the D is for David, my dad, David Marshall Lloyd Griffiths. It's a miniature tribute to him for all the wisdom he has shared with me throughout my life.

As for Gran, her persona is my personal requiem for never having been to my grandparents' funerals. There's a bit of each of my grandparents in Gran's character.

The character Mom is based on my own mother, Jean Ann Griffiths. A little note of thanks to the woman who raised me as best she could; I was a full-time kid.

Art represents my brother, Arthur Gordon Griffiths. In Canada, we have a saying: "Friends are the family you choose." The best choice I never had to make. Thank goodness for that.

Sensei Iura is a name I've drawn from my childhood friend, Takashei Iura.

As for the rest of the people in Jin's story, many of them are based on myself (I'll never tell which parts), and the others are based on various experiences that emphasized any given point about great salesmanship.

I've been asked what's it like to write a book, and I always respond with "I've no idea."

On occasion, the question has then turned to "How do you go about writing a book?" As this book comes to its close, the experience has led me to believe that the greatest challenge has been within myself, allowing the creative juices to flow in exploring my own creativity.

Though very spiritual, I'm not a particularly religious person, so please understand the depth of my sincerity when I explain the sensation of having to give myself to something outside of myself in order to allow the spirit to come to me.

"The words I found therein, the courage to write them I find thereout." Some people may translate or interpret this as having given myself to one or another god of their belief, for which I have no objection as long as it helps their understanding my answer.

I have given my understanding to paper, which has become this work and encompasses the basics of the sales process based on fourteen years' experience in the field while consistently delivering extraordinary results.

Lastly, no written work is complete until read, and I'd like to thank you, the reader, for helping me complete that process.

Thank you,

Jason

a.k.a.: bigdamnjason@me.com

Appendix B

The Eight Steps of Selling

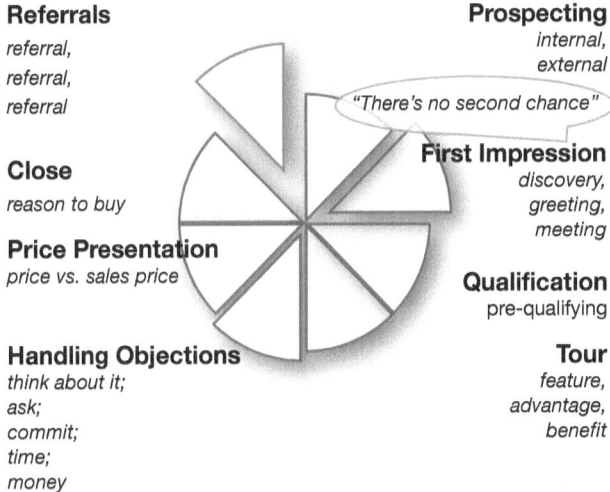

There's nothing "new" about the eight steps of selling.

Like the slices of a well made pie, each slice is a part of the whole. Leave a slice out and the whole is much more difficult to put together.

Herein, each slice is considered a tool. Understanding each tool's applications are key in completing the whole sales process. The order each tool is approached needn't always be clockwise.

For example, handling objections during the qualifying step not only deflects the chance of an objection slicing the deal, but it furthers rapport towards getting referrals.

Appendix C

Considered Sources

Etiquette and Custom in Kenya
Meeting and Greeting

The most common greeting is the handshake.

When greeting someone with whom you have a personal relationship, the handshake is more prolonged than the one given to a casual acquaintance.

Close female friends may hug and kiss once on each cheek instead of shaking hands.

When greeting an elder or someone of higher status, grasp the right wrist with the left hand while shaking hands to demonstrate respect.

Muslim men/women do not always shake hands with women/men.

The most common greeting is "Jambo?" ("How are you?"), which is generally said immediately prior to the handshake.

After the handshake it is the norm to ask questions about their health, their family, business, and anything else you know about the person.

To skip or rush this element in the greeting process is the height of poor manners.

Source: http://www.kwintessential.co.uk/resources/global-etiquette/kenya.html.

The Origins of the Common Handshake

The handshake has become a common form of communication all around the world. It is used to say "hello," "good-bye," "we agree," as a greeting upon first acquaintance, and as a mutual sign of goodwill and peace. A handshake can establish a first impression with someone, whether it be good and firm, or limp and clammy. The handshake has made its way to the highest levels of government and society where agreements between nations are sealed. This ritual has "become perhaps our most important nonverbal communicative contrivance."

But where did it come from?

There are many conflicting reports of the possible source of the common handshake gesture. Some say that it originated in medieval times with the etiquette of knights; others say it appeared later in the courts of British nobles in colonial times. Still others say it dates to the Romans who would approach each other and grab the forearm to make sure the other man was not carrying a weapon. **Most agree, however, that the handshake predates written history, and is therefore somewhat difficult to track down**. The earliest records we have of the handshake are from the Egyptians:

The Egyptian hieroglyphic of the extended hand represents the verb, "to give." **This symbol finds its derivation in the shaking of hands that represented the legend of the handing over of power from a god to an early [earthly?] ruler**. Hence the Babylonian ritual (circa 1800 BC) in which the king clasped the hand of a statue (the god Marduk) during the New Year's festival so that his authority was transferred to the next year. When Babylon fell to the Assyrians, hands kept right on shaking, with the new kings carrying on the ancient ritual for fear of offending the gods.

Some claim that it is the Egyptian hieroglyph of the extended hand that inspired Michelangelo when he painted his famed fresco *The Creation of Adam* in the Sistine Chapel. In it, Adam stretches forth his hand toward God's hand.

Another source tells us more about how the ancients viewed the hand symbolically:

In esoteric doctrine, the position of the hand in relation to the body, and the arrangement of the fingers, convey certain precise symbolic notions ... two hands joined signifies mystic marriage ... according to Berber thought, the hand signifies protection, authority, power, and strength.

Source: http://www.templestudy.com/2008/02/07/the-origin-of-the-common-handshake/.

Appendix D

DISC Analysis

DISC analysis is a method of quick personality assessment for the black-belt salesperson. Though no two people are alike, adjusting a sales style when approaching a prospect to appeal to his or her main DISC characteristic can aid in building rapport and avoiding confrontation.

D: Dominant—The direct person; the extra-firm handshake; the three-piece suit; the controller who seeks to pursue the sale on his or her terms. *Assure dominant people you understand their time is valuable and you are not there to waste it.* Fear of having the time to do or deal with the salesperson is the most common objection for the dominant type.

I: Impulsive—The spontaneous people; brightly colored shoes and clothing, and bling, are common indicators. *Assuring them of how their decision is going to make them feel is key when dealing with this personality type.*

S: Secure—The more introverted or reserved type. *Assurances of a company's history and longevity are key in addressing secure people's most common objection of commitment.* Fear of commitment is often a sign of prospects requiring more security.

C: Cautious—Pocket protectors, calculators, and geek or nerdish types are associated with the C-type. Typically these types find great personal reward in accounting positions. *Have the actual data necessary to support their decision.*

Individuals are not usually one or the other personality type, but combinations of them. Each individual has a unique combination of qualities that can be expressed, as seen in Chart D1.

Uppercase and lowercase letters indicate the main and secondary characteristics.

Chart D1

TYPE	d	i	s	c
D	D	Di	Ds	Dc
I	Id	I	Is	Ic
S	Sd	Si	S	Sc
C	Cd	Ci	Cs	C

Certain combinations are less likely to occur but are not impossible. A "dominant cautious" type would seem as unlikely as a "cautious dominant" type, but they are not unheard of.

Others may *want* to be the dominant type so much that it may be difficult to initially see their true type. Establishing rapport will clarify what types are actually in play.

The black-belt salesperson may opt to appeal to one or more DISC types, to remove objections before they even come about.

www.ingramcontent.com/pod-product-compliance
Lightning Source LLC
Chambersburg PA
CBHW030924180526
45163CB00002B/457